Physician, Heal Thyself

Mary Russell

in collaboration with Lisa Sand MD

Physician, Heal Thyself

ISBN 186163

Cover design by Paul Mason

Published by:

Capall Bann Publishing
Freshfields
Chieveley
Berks
RG20 8TF

Contents

Other Titles by the authors, also published by Capall Bann:

Vortex - The End of History by Mary Russell

Medicine For the Coming Age by Dr Lisa Sand

Foreword

This is the healing time.

Bathed in love emanating from the very heart of All and everything, this Earth humanity is finding that its old hurts, its old fears, its deepest pains have the chance to dissolve in that great balm of universal healing.

And everywhere that that love is being accepted and the chance is being taken, what was once so pressing and so urgent and so terrible is slipping away into nothingness.

But where the love reaches and is not accepted, then there is a chasm which opens up and into which those who will not take what is freely and lovingly offered will slip in their pursuit of a different destiny.

Recognise what is happening, and see the part in the great process occurring which you are also playing, both through healing yourselves and healing others.

Wherever there was a wound, wherever there was a hurt, there will be a new growth, a flower of joy.

This comes with love from a Universe which loves this planet and all those upon it.

April 1999

Introduction

There is a long and winding road that you embark upon when you deny your true nature, your reality. It is a road that has been followed by the majority of this Earth's humanity for many thousands of years. It has led through injustice and war, through slavery and suppression; it has resulted in a long, slow diminution of the joy and wonder of being alive to emotionality, and artificiality, and false values which are now everywhere like a cancer in the human soul.

It has progressed to the point that Earth's peoples distrust themselves so completely that they even deny the existence of the Creator and of their own in-dwelling soul. They turn their backs on the opportunities for joy and laughter; they turn away from the path of their own fulfilment; they ignore the ever-present guidance of the divine spark within them that urges them towards progress and positivity.

Denial of who they are, of their essential unity with each other and All there is, is so embedded in the Earth population that they believe their misery, their confusion, their illness, their anxiety and anger, and their run-down, polluted world, with its strife and tensions, to be normal. They believe that this is how it is meant to be and that all their problems will be solved by the latest scientific research, by the most recent peace initiative, by the most impressive promise of a future which will be very different from the past, but which never arrives as they hope.

They deny themselves and then they wonder why they don't feel good, why they are so stressed, so tired, why they get so ill. They wonder why their fellows take drugs, and abuse their children, why they rob and cheat and torture and kill. They cannot understand why nothing seems to help the poverty and the suffering they see on their television and in their newspapers. They feel guilty and send their money to help.

But they would do better to keep their money and look inside themselves if they want to change the world, if they want to change their own lives.

People of Earth, in turning away from your true reality, which is that each of you is an eternal Spirit which has taken on physical incarnation, you yourselves have made the world as it is. Had you accepted your own nature and lived in harmony with the divine within you, your world would be a Paradise, lush and fertile, bright with all manner of beautiful creatures and flowers and abundant in the bounty it would offer you, its inhabitants. That bounty would include a temperate climate, more than enough to sustain life, and the yielding up of secrets that you might use to create the structures and tools necessary for your enjoyment, and to feed your curiosity and creativity - all without pollution, without degradation of resources, without side-effects or any of the other unwanted consequences of "civilisation".

You would be living in harmony not only with your own body, with your eternal Self and with your fellow human beings, but also with the rest of creation; you would be at one with your planet, and with the Universe and all the other humanities in it. You would be living in harmony with the eternal, with the timeless, with the creative - and what possibilities would open up to you of knowledge beyond anything you can imagine, and creative achievement beyond all your science fiction!

As a people you are by now so far descended into the material, that for many of you these words mean nothing. You cannot imagine life other than what is known and familiar to you, and you seek to assuage the longing in you through false security, through routines and security, through family, food, money, sex, power and position - or through rebellion against any and all of the above - and through the mind-numbing banality of your entertainment and so-called culture.

But it has been making you ill, and as long as you deny the in-dwelling Spirit you can never feel well nor free nor truly joyful.
This is not to say that none of you who read these words accept the truth. Indeed, those of you who are struggling to set aside the

lure and power of the emotions and the intellect are many. Only those who seek to embrace the light they feel deep, deep within their being, or who already know that light, would wish to read a book such as this.

For those of you who embrace the light find that your lives are transformed. It might be step by step, or in a great rush of incoming positivity. It happens just as the soul is ready for it and can accept it. Symptoms vanish, emotions calm down under the ascendancy of the Spirit, and the whole being lights up from within as you find out at last what it feels like to be truly alive and to know that life is truly wonderful.

Until the soul sets itself upon such a path, there can be no well-being and no real joy; nor can there be any real possibility of making a meaningful contribution to the world. For as a soul lights up, its light radiates around the planet on a level of great power far above that of the material. From that level it lifts not just the individual, but the condition of the planet itself and of all those upon it who are themselves ready to make a change.

No other contribution can achieve as much. Nothing else will serve to improve, to change, to transform the condition of the individual or his planet.

This book is for all of you true souls who wish to find the light within, or whose aim is to help others to find their light. It is time for those upon this planet to stop their headlong flight from themselves. It is time for them to turn around and open their minds, to open their hearts and let go of all their false crutches, all their "security blankets" on the material level, all their ingrained thoughts and habits and attitudes. It is time for them to let go their fear, their anxiety, their hatred and dissatisfaction and stand in the light which is the light of the love of the Universe. It is time for them to let that love show them what is true and good and beautiful and real and joyful.

We whose world is the light stand by to help all of you who know this too. We stand by to make you aware that you and we are one and the same, that all is One, that all is light. Light is increasing all over the darkened globe of the planet because of the efforts of you and those like you. It will not be so long until there is a great change and a new world will come into being in which peace reigns and all live in Oneness.

We give you these writings that they may help you in the work you and we are doing together, even if you are not always aware of it, to bring the new world into being.

7/6/99

NB
All communications recently received, especially where reference is made to specific events or developments, are dated

Chapter 1

Identity

Truth is simple.

There is more truth in a humble ant and in a grain of rice than in all the religions of the world, all institutions or all legislations.

The ant and the seed simply are what they are, without any ands, ifs or buts. They follow their innermost urges to perfection and instantly, without question or doubt. They do not worry about yesterday or tomorrow.

The present moment is the only time they recognise. In it, they recognise themselves as part and parcel of All there is. In their respective costumes they simply fulfil themselves and their calling.

A similar attitude would bring health, joy and peace to this Earth humanity, and that is its birthright.

April 1999

1.1 Finding Yourself

Stand in front of a mirror and look at what you see in it. Feel your arms and legs; say your name in full.

Then sit down comfortably and quietly to consider who and what you are.

In school, you learned that all matter consists of atoms. Your body is matter. Your brain is part of it. Between the atoms constituting your body there are huge spaces. Physics teaches that if you could compact all the atoms of your body together so that there would be no space between them, they would all fit comfortably onto the head of a pin.

If that way of looking at your physical being is uncomfortable, just wait. It gets worse.

For an atom is not solid either. Like a sun and its planets, the atom has a nucleus round which circle one or more electrons at a considerable distance, relatively speaking. The solidity of atoms is equally illusory as the solidity of matter. Constituents of atoms have long been recognised to be particles in name only.

To us the human attitude towards anything composed of matter is absolutely hilarious. Seen from our point of view it is pure thought which can be transmuted into form or, wrongly manipulated, become a distorted image of its true origin.

The three-dimensional image of matter is perceived as real only by others of similar nature. It is indeed a 'virtual reality'.

Sooner or later, man in general will have to have his being on a higher level from which he can judge clearly the illusion in which he has had his being until now.

1.2 What are the Characteristics of Wholeness and Well-being?

Wholeness, which is also wholesomeness, and well-being are what every human being aspires to, whether consciously or deeper in himself than he has allowed his conscious mind to penetrate.

They are simply a sense of rightness and ease and joy about being Self. They include the peace and contentment which come from a sure connection and identification with who and what he really is. With this identification, there is no place or need for thinking or worrying about Self, or about dealings with others, or about the challenges of living.

In other words, wholeness is simply being. It is accepting Self as it is and enjoying being Self. It is allowing the true Self within to guide and direct from its high and objective viewpoint which sees the whole where the limited intellect can see only the part. This is the true humility by which the temporary or little self accepts the ascendancy of the eternal Self and allows it to express itself through its earthly vehicle in a supreme partnership.

Wholeness is oneness with the true Self which continues when the body dies, and which existed before the body was formed. Wholeness is where the personality relaxes into the arms of the loving Spirit and, safely held by that which is eternal and One with everything else, gladly reflects its light in the material world.

Wholeness is where the personality accepts its true identity as Spirit, and identifies with it without reservation. It identifies with the joy, the strength, the deep abiding peace and love, and the supreme confidence and capability which characterise the eternal Self. It identifies with the eternal, with the infinite and with the purpose of the Divine within it, and as such it knows its true being as part of all the Universe and all Creation.

Life lived from a knowledge of belonging with All and everything is pure joy and enjoyment emanating from a deep inner peace; it is glad acceptance of the learning, the challenges and opportunities, and the adventures of incarnation. Identified with the Spirit, what the personality expresses is all love and compassion, all light and truth, all strength and gladness. Radiating light and guided by the inspiration of the eternal Spirit, much can be achieved by the incarnation and much brought to a world which needs its positivity so greatly. This is being, and it is utterly natural everywhere, except on your planet.

Knowing Self as part of and integral to the whole of Creation is the source of the greatest security there can be. You on Earth sense this in your rare moments of illumination when, transported by the beauty of a landscape or a sunset or beautiful music, you let down your defences and find yourselves flooded with the sense that all is absolutely right and well just as it is, that everything is as it should be and that you yourselves are just fine.

In such moments, brief though they are, you are open to and accept what is known and accepted on a continuing basis by all other human beings in the Universe. This is what we mean by wholeness. And in a state of wholeness the entire being, including the physical being, is lifted up and becomes light and easy and utterly well.
The rebellion against wholeness which characterises Earth humanity down the ages results in an identification with the material rather than the spiritual, with untruth rather than truth.

Neither the material nor the lie can sustain a state of joy and peace and harmony. The opposite is in fact the case, and this misidentification is the source of all disharmony and disease in your world today. It is a stance which diverts and absorbs huge amounts of emotional energy just to maintain it. In such a state of being it is almost impossible to feel relaxed or easy or peaceful; nor is there much scope or room for joy or for love.

Instead, while identification with the reality of the Spirit brings peace and joy and certainty, identification with the pseudo-reality of the material brings insecurity and fear and tremendous frustration and alienation. Without its anchor in reality the population of the planet has opened the door to negativity in all its most virulent and abhorrent forms.

This is the basis of life on Earth. It is as you can see a complete crisis of identity. And this brings about a state in the population which can only be understood as post-traumatic stress disorder. This is the basis of nearly all disease as we shall discuss more fully further on.

Today, the anxiety is so great that disease is ever more rife, despite the much vaunted technological advances of recent times. There is no true remedy in any drug or technique that can be dreamt up in any laboratory. The real diseases of this humanity are not of the body. They are of the soul, and for real cure there is only one possibility - to embrace the true Self and allow it to guide and direct the incarnation according to the natural order of the Universe.

15/10/98

1.3 Mind, Body, Spirit

In order to better understand the nature of disease, it is essential to fully recognise that you have your being on three levels - body, mind, and Spirit.

The body together with the mind is, if you like, the earthly representative of the Spirit. Communicating with the body through the mind, the Spirit has the opportunity to accomplish specific aims and aspirations on the material level. Without them it can achieve nothing.

Without the Spirit, the body/mind is adrift, purposeless and afraid. It is prey to material forces, including its own emotions. Lacking its link with its Source it attempts to compensate through the material, through money, power, sex and so on, but nothing can satisfy the deep longing within it except reunion with the animating, life-giving true Self.

Thus, as you can see, the three levels interact one with another. When they are in harmony, then all is well and the human being is healthy, not just physically but also emotionally, mentally and spiritually.

Physically the immune system is able to operate without constraint so that it keeps the body safe from the many bacteria and viruses that would attack it. It is able to do so because, being under the ascendancy of the higher Self, the emotions and the mind are at peace. When they are not at peace, they attack the immune system in the first place so that it is weakened and unable to fight off further attack.

It is a sad fact that a state of harmony is rare on this planet. In truth, the vast majority of humankind on Earth is out of harmony with itself. This is to say that these people do not accept themselves as they truly are and do not love themselves. They reject their true nature and will have nothing to do with who and what it is they actually are. They allow the mind or the emotions to usurp the supremacy of the Spirit, so that where there was peace and love and joy, strife and anxiety and disharmony reign in their stead.

It is from this disharmony that there arises the whole gamut of emotional, behavioural and physical disorders.

12/8/98

Chapter 2

Illness

2.1 What is Illness?

When conflicting thoughts and emotions become intolerable, the individual sets up a symptom or disease process. This serves to distract the personality by focusing its attention, at least in part, onto another line.

This well-known fact is best illustrated by some of the old popular pronouncements, such as something or someone is a pain in the neck, when a person is confronted by an apparently unsolvable situation: "Oh, my aching back!" "What a headache!" is another one.

While these comments are applied to obvious and outer circumstances and happenings, the chief culprits are inner ones.

Fear and anger tend to lead to usually inappropriate action or paralysis which can be graphically clinical or express as passivity.

The inappropriate action can be directed at other people or damage the person's own body and its functions. One thing is certain: it is rarely what it appears to be, viewed in a superficial way. The old song has much truth in it: "Row, row, row your boat gently down the stream; merrily, merrily, merrily, merrily, life is but a dream."

Dreams are symbolic in all their details, and so are illness and inappropriate behaviour patterns.

There is no such thing as a coincidence and all is plain to see when the truth behind it is known. What looks like calamity turns out to be opportunity for the soul to progress in a direction which it has hitherto resisted. This resistance, which plagues earth man so much - even whole nations - can easily be seen to spring from deep-seated fear and rage, causing a holding on to old, outworn patterns of thought, expression and behaviour, reminiscent of the proverbial donkey with its hooves dug in.

When, eventually, the fallacy is seen for what it is, it can easily be relinquished with a laugh rather than with a whimper.

Life is there to be lived rather than to be suffered. But if people insist on suffering, they are free to court it.

2.2 All Disease Comes from the Soul

No true practice of medicine can take place without recognising the fundamental truth that all disease proceeds from the soul.

Without this understanding and acceptance of the nature of disease, medical practice is confined to the treatment of symptoms while the underlying cause is barely tackled, if at all.

In this context, the prevalence and rise of illness and disease in modern times can only make sense in terms of the outlook and life-style of modern humanity. Were scientific advance the only criterion, all disease should have been eradicated decades ago. Indeed, for a while it seemed that it would be, just as today it seems that the new discipline of genetics will solve all the ills of humankind.

Yet illness and disease are still rife, still threaten. After 200 years of modern science, asthma in children is on the increase, cancer and heart disease are still killers, and new diseases such as Aids have appeared. Even old diseases such as TB, thought to have been brought under control, are making a comeback.

All this is testimony to the existence of other factors. It is instructive to note the decimation of native populations in, for example, South America, when exposed to members of the so-called "civilised" nations. This happened not just at the time of the Spanish Conquest, but happens today as well wherever previously isolated tribes come into contact with modern civilisation - and its diseases.

Such examples suggest that civilisation is not a step forward, but a step back. What are anxiety and Aids for example but diseases arising out of life-style? And where does that life-style with its obsession with time and drugs and sex and adrenaline originate if not in the desperation and longing of souls caught in a deep crisis of identity?

It will be only when medicine and humanity as a whole recognise and understand that the entire population of planet Earth is caught in a massive and traumatising identity crisis that true medical practice can take place.

True medical practice aims to heal the trauma in the soul from which disease arises. As a real understanding of disease becomes common knowledge, then medical practice will come into its own as maintenance of health and prevention of disease, even accidents, by concentrating on the healthy mind, arising from identification with Self, which will keep the body healthy also.

30/7/98

2.3 Post-Traumatic Stress Disorder

"Bah" wails the new-born when it has pulled some air into its lungs, is held by its feet to drain the air passages and/or is slapped on its little behind to make it cry and expand its lungs.

What a shocking welcome!

And these customary procedures are carried out by unfamiliar and detached strangers.

Imagine the feelings! You've probably been looking forward to your time in an Earth body, and then you are punished for having come!

Other attacks on your peace and joy have probably already preceded your birth, and many more will follow it. Let us take a look at some of them.

Mother, herself quite immature: “I hope I don’t get pregnant”; or, having missed a period: “I’m pregnant. I’m terrified. I don’t want a baby. What am I going to do?”

You know that you are going in where you are not wanted. You have your reasons for doing so, but once in that environment you have forgotten them and you are terrified. You feel trapped, exiled and helpless. You have come from a sphere where communication is by thought, not word, and no thought is hidden. For a long time yet you will perceive thought and feeling rather than words. You will send signals of love and receive none in return. Your sense of isolation and confusion will deepen.

Much of the time while your body is developing in mother’s uterus you will, though connected to the body, return to the sphere from which you have come to fortify and strengthen yourself for the life you have chosen. To human perception you will simply be asleep.

You could say that you are like a cordless telephone. In order to keep on functioning, you must return to base frequently to recharge your battery. This is, in fact, something you and everyone else will be doing throughout life on Earth.

The “cordlessness” is apparent, not real. You do actually exist on two levels, though you have probably lost the awareness of the fact.

The absence of love, the repeated experiencing of terror, the development of confusion and fear in the mortal personality cause an abnormally intense identification with the physical self and the material world around it, so that any sense of your true reality is pushed far into the background, away from the outer consciousness.

A desperate struggle to hold body and soul together takes precedence over all else. The natural state of peace, harmony and

joy is over-shadowed by a sad and angry despair.
As the incoming soul is shocked into an abnormal identification with its earthly condition, its trust in itself and its own truth is shattered. It is, in fact, hypnotised by the shocking events into an entirely faulty self-image of weakness, vulnerability and lack of worth.

The soul, and with it the personality, has acquired post-traumatic stress disorder already before birth in very many instances. Amnesia for the shocking events follows, but the hypnotic suggestions they planted remain and need to be recognised and removed at a later time, with the full co-operation of the sufferer.

2.4 Bonding

The soul associates itself with a fertilised ovum. This, the first cell making up the human body, already contains the entire blueprint of its subsequent development. This plan consists of the genes contributed by both parents

Early on, the soul becomes aware of all that occurs in and around the chosen mother, especially her thoughts and emotions. In associating more closely with the growing body, the soul loses a good part of its knowledge of its own individuality, feeling itself as part of the mother. This is especially true when untoward circumstances come about which confuse or shock the incoming being.

As long as love and harmony prevail, the little one feels safe and secure. When, however, emotions of fear, anger, hate, resentment, guilt or rebellion exist in the parents, these prevent or shut off the free flow of love which is so essential for normal development. If mother is attacked in any way or undermined, or if she cannot keep her own temper under loving control, the little one suffers shock.

Any wish or thought of having an abortion, for example, is perceived as the threat of annihilation, the total condemnation of the incoming soul for even existing. Any and all of these experiences, especially when they have been more than momentary or when they take place repeatedly, leave open wounds or scars on the personality of the child. Unless they heal smoothly, with or without "plastic surgery" at some time during the life, they influence the state of being and the decision-making for a lifetime.

If mother and father are harmonious in themselves and truly love each other, welcoming the chance to give other souls the opportunity to incarnate, the unborn child is well bonded. Bonding is simply true love. It is not the spurious emotionality so commonly espoused as love in popular music and literature. It is not passion which is known to evaporate or turn to anger and disappointment in a short time. Neither is it the intense feeling of need which is only very temporarily satisfied by close association through sexual contact.

These states are, in fact, evidence of a parent's own infantile deficit which has left the personality in a condition of more or less permanent childhood.

True love is a calm, cheerful, optimistic state of being based on real appreciation of Self and a sense of self-value. On a deep feeling level it is the automatic awareness of the spiritual identity of the person himself and that of others. This supplies a profound feeling of essential wholeness and invulnerability. The individual is conscious of being himself but is not self-conscious. He is free and enjoys grappling with the opportunities and challenges life brings. To such a one, change means progress rather than threat, whatever outward appearances may suggest.

The importance of pre-natal bonding, although known, is often not sufficiently appreciated. Knowing of it places the responsibility of seeing to his or her personality's maturity before tackling parenthood squarely on the shoulders of the prospective parent.

A true adult does not yearn for sexual satisfaction with the intensity of a starving person's longing for food, or with a lecherous demand for satisfying an appetite which, as you can see,

is essentially insatiable.
These yearnings and demands simply express the love-starved, rejected inner child's angry demand for satisfaction.

A real adult is by the very nature of the indwelling Spirit creative. This creativity expresses itself quite naturally and easily in everyday life, whatever the individual's chosen path and destiny may be. With childhood safely out of the way, the present moment and activity is enjoyed, and even the person's own state is useful and constructive.

There is then a balance in all things. This balance is a long way from perfectionism which, in fact, inhibits any free unfolding of creativity. Perfectionism is clear evidence of an underlying lack of self-esteem. Free-flowing creativity brings the satisfaction of accomplishment and self-fulfilment which enables the true adult to be objective and sufficiently perceptive to distinguish positive from negative. It is not easy for anyone else to pull the wool over the eyes of a really grown-up individual because the inner sense of truth is functioning to capacity.

The children of genuinely adult parents are bound to be well-bonded. They are therefore miles ahead on the road to self-fulfilment.

However, depending on what the path is which the incarnating soul has selected for itself, it may be of advantage to have built poor or absent bonding into the childhood pattern. If, for example, the soul wishes to be in a position of helping others to find their wholeness after a disturbed or deficient early experience, it would not be possible to have the necessary empathic understanding of the consequences of such damage if that soul had not experienced and overcome similar damage itself.

Only through having fought the battle and won it, can a person successfully teach others to do the same.

Man can only learn through example, step by step. Conversely, he can only teach what he has learned himself through experience.

Two examples

The most common situation in which modern man finds himself is not that of disruption of his wholeness, but that of a lack of wholeness from the beginning.

As a tiny baby, a new human life is at its most defenceless and vulnerable. For its survival to be assured and, even more importantly from the point of view of the new being, for it to feel that its survival is assured, it must be surrounded by the unconditional love of the parents or important adults. Where unconditional love is lacking, so too are the conditions for the child to develop in harmony with its true nature as an eternal Spirit.

This is not the fault of the parents. Where they too have come into the world or grown up without unconditional love, they are then not capable of giving what they do not have themselves to their children.

Thus are the "sins" of the fathers visited on the children, from generation to generation. The following examples show how this process occurs.

Human beings on Earth are born into an imperfect world. Actually, you have already been steeped in it for nine months before you take your first breath of air. Let no-one make the mistake of thinking that you are not profoundly affected by this pre-natal time.

You were knowledgeable beings before you entered your present body, and you were far from unconscious during its development. That permanent being which is aware of its selfhood is the soul.

Let us give you the example of Maria, a middle-aged lady. She had suffered nearly all her life from constipation, and worried about it, off and on. Yet medical examinations never revealed any abnormality. Nor had changes in diet brought any relief.

However, a brief review of the earliest part of her life revealed that her mother had had a prolonged labour giving birth to Maria - her first-born. The mother was very frightened of birthing, being herself an anxious person. The unborn child was surrounded by her mother's fear. Terrified of death or damage from the birth, the mother was holding back the process with the result that the baby was terrorised.

This state, maintained during a two-day labour, had a hypnotic effect on the unborn baby's consciousness. It formed an imprint, or engram, in the little one's mind, long before the brain was capable of thinking rationally.

At this early stage, the new personality could not feel itself as truly separate from mother, nor totally a part of her. This made the presence of strong, sustained, negative emotions like fear and anger very confusing.

From the first day of existence outside her mother's body, Maria had the experience of bowel movements. These would remind her strongly of her mother's labour. Later in life, circumstances or emotions would trigger the deeply buried memory and Maria would find herself re-enacting her mother's behaviour during labour, of holding back, not letting go.

The daughter became constipated and did not know why. She had to learn to love herself, her soul, her all, so that she could lose her fear and relax in daily life. Her body then was able to perform its functions smoothly, without interference from her thoughts.

It is a simple fact that strong, negative emotion interferes with the free flow of love. The mother's increasing dread during her pregnancy was perceived by the little one as fear of her when what she needed for normal development was love. Thus, whenever in later life Maria's anxiety level rose for a while she automatically imitated her mother's holding back.

The root trouble was that Maria's high anxiety meant that she was unable to love and accept herself; she could not relax and be natural in her daily life and feeling.

Another example was Tom. His mother was also a worrier. The undertone of anger in her feelings was not lost on her baby, who responded in kind. As a new-born he learned that he could worry his mother if he held back his bowel movements. She expected them to occur with clock-like regularity. The baby derived a certain satisfaction from her fussing and from the sense of power his withholding gave him.

Later in life, when a situation stimulated his old anger, he became constipated but did not know why. The infantile experience had long fallen prey to amnesia.

2.5 Immunity - Two Case Histories

Gerald, a self-employed businessman, came down with a nasty 'flu. There was a lot of it about but Gerald, though much exposed to the sneezing and coughing of others, had not caught anything all winter, until this day. Then it hit him with a vengeance.

He was devastated. He badly needed to take care of his business and consulted a spiritual psychotherapist, knowing there was more to it than simply catching a "bug".

On being prompted to come up with an incident in which he was deeply upset by something or someone in the week before he became ill, he remembered that a friend he had trusted had let him down badly in a project that was of great importance.

He had held up despite his disappointment. However, subconsciously, the incident had reminded him of his childhood, of a time when his father left home and his mother had to fend for herself and the children. It was a tremendous shock to the child, and the recent experience had cued him back into it without his being consciously aware of the fact.

The re-living of that feeling of a treasonable abandonment, of the outrage, the helplessness, the despair of the child, undermined his immune system. It could not function with its accustomed efficiency.

The little boy in Gerald's subconscious was angry at the absent father. As he could not hit out at his real father, he turned on the internalised father, his own inner self. The immune system cannot stand such attacks. It becomes temporarily paralysed, or starts to attack the very body of which it is a part.

A brief illustration of the last-mentioned fact is Karl, who on occasion was heard by his wife to say: "I hate myself", with real venom. No-one doubted that Karl was in a very negative state.

When he was fifty years old, he was diagnosed as having one of the severely disabling neurologic diseases for which there is no cure. Two years later he died. He had never wanted to change. His true immortal Self could do no more with the ultra-negative personality.

Gerald recovered after enough bed rest, and in time became so firmly identified with his inner, spiritual Self that he no longer reran the old recording.

Yet Karl brightened up substantially as his end obviously neared. This often happens when the joy of the soul at going home from its incarnation is so strong that it breaks through the rebellion of the weakening earthly personality. Outright joy or a joyful serenity takes over.

There are also many instances in which the soul has left some time before physical death occurs. In these cases, if the patient is conscious, there can be an apparent personality change. A previously meek or well-mannered individual may suddenly speak in foul language and be thoroughly unreasonable and aggressive. In other instances, a charming, vivacious person becomes dull, listless and boring for a time before physical death.

In both instances, it is easy to see that the change is brought about by the withdrawal of the animating force, the eternal Self, leaving only a personality.

2.6 The Lack of Love

The point must be made in the strongest possible terms.

Loving acceptance of Self from the start allows an individual to proceed, from the very beginning of his physical, emotional and spiritual development and experience, on the basis of inner security and self-esteem. This inner security and self-esteem come from a clear sense of identification of the new personality with its source, the eternal Spirit.

On such a basis all development unfolds as necessary for the well-being of the incarnation.

On planet Earth loving acceptance of Self is far from the norm. It is almost completely absent. Where there is no loving acceptance of Self, the necessary unfolding of each developmental stage cannot take place as it should. The infant's emotional development becomes arrested at a very early point.There is a schism between the Self and its new personality right from the start. It is this schism which is the root cause of "all the ills that flesh is heir to".

How this comes about is a direct consequence of the inability of the important adults in the child's life to give the unconditional love and loving environment that it needs, even whilst in the womb. This deficit sets up a fear state in the new incarnation. From this state of fear, other states arise: desperate need for the unconditional love that is not forthcoming; frustration at the repeated failure of sometimes heroic efforts to win the love it needs which will allay the fear; despair, rage and rebellion.

With yet more experience as the infant grows, another layer of negative emotions comes about: resentment, especially where demands are made of the little one without the reward it seeks; jealousy, where a sibling is perceived to receive more love, attention, recognition or understanding; even aggression, rebellion and vindictiveness where anger predominates; or lack of confidence, passivity, self-sacrifice, self-sabotage and in the worst cases self-destruction; or mixtures of these, as well as other negatively-focused examples of outlook and behaviour such as cynicism and indifference.

For where there is little or no love of Self, the new being is vulnerable not only to the traumas and deficiencies of its early life, but its difficulties may also cue it into past-life conditioning and unresolved emotions from previous incarnations, where these are similar - and they often are. These come into play in the current incarnation, which offers them a stage on which to replay the past in an attempt to seek resolution in so doing.

Outlook and behaviour are generally recognised to have an influence upon health even in these ignorant times. It is accepted that so-called stress leads to illness. But it is still not fully recognised that all illness arises out of inner states of being. Where the emotions are out of kilter, the thought content is inevitably affected, and where thought runs riot, both behaviour and physical being reflect the chaos within.

Some individuals manage to achieve a certain accommodation with their afflictions and make progress despite them, especially as experience enables them to gain some insight into what is going on. These people usually have some awareness of their inner reality which acts as a guide and help.

Others however are firmly stuck at the point of the original trauma itself. They repeat rigidly and endlessly the same thoughts, the same emotional patterns, the same behaviour, and this, sooner or later, brings about physical consequences.

In such cases it must be realised that the Spirit is not a passive onlooker. The aim of the Spirit is to express itself in all its glory through the incarnation. To do this it must find the way to free the vehicle - that is the body and its personality with its emotions and mind - from what hampers and obstructs its aims and expression. Wherever there is hope of breaking free sufficiently from the aberrant emotions and faulty conditioning at the root of the schism, the Spirit will do whatever it takes.

At some times no action is required. It is enough to let the personality run with its highly disagreeable emotional load, and experience the direct consequences of its inability to accept the direction and guidance of the indwelling Self in its everyday life.

At other times, when the personality is endangering the very soul itself, the Spirit will help to bring about shocks designed to jolt the personality out of its dangerous tendencies. It will employ changes of circumstances, events, losses, symptoms (which are not always signs of full-blown disease), even accidents to try and get its message across.

Where a personality will not alter, the emotional wear and tear will affect the body itself, the basic resource of the Spirit in incarnation. In many instances, a heart attack or a cancer may provide enough of a shock to bring about a change of outlook. In other instances where the condition is more of a chronic nature such as arthritis, or back pain, the condition itself will mirror what the individual is doing to himself. The disease or illness is never a haphazard occurrence: it arises out of a particular emotional blockage and faithfully reflects the nature of its cause.

Healing can occur in almost all except the most extreme cases where the Spirit has decided that there is nothing further it can achieve with the current incarnation.

But for true healing to occur, the cause of the illness must be addressed rather than the symptoms.

12/8/98

2.7 The Disease of Egotism

Society as you know it is characterised by a state of communal egotism instead of "letting go" and realising the communal soul. This is an appalling fact which applies to families, to communities, to countries, to nations and to the entire world today.

The cause of this lack of generosity towards one another lies in the preponderant development of the "ego" or personal "I" into a malignant growth. The true "I" is the eye of the soul; the false "I" a morbid centre for the cancerous growth of egotistical separation.

Only when the diseased state of this false "ego" has been recognised will man, as an individual in a community, and nations, as a world-wide community, see the depths to which humankind has sunk in its spiritual awareness and understanding.

Herein lies the great failure of man to come to terms with himself and his true nature. And being on a level of utter ignorance in regard to the Law of Cause and Effect, he will consequently attract to himself, from the pool of negativity, all that which will eventually cause him to sink into a morass of futility, hopelessness, lethargy and despair.

We would call you to attention, beloved ones, and ask you to meditate on these thoughts and let your true Self revive in you the knowledge of eternal life and the exact and perfect laws of all Creation. In exercising the mind to "tune in" to the harmony of the heavenly spheres, you will create for yourselves a perfect habitat of peace through the correct use of positive thought. In this manner your entire being will be enveloped by the love and wisdom of the ageless divinity within yourselves. And from the measureless Source of this well of being, you will find that understanding which will enable you to become a channel for the out-flowing of the waters of love-wisdom, to realise peace and perfect living on Earth.

If you are willing to learn we will teach you. An open mind is like the tilled earth, prepared and ready to receive the seed which will eventually take root and sprout. And the picture it will present at the time of fruition will be pleasing to the eye and strengthening to all those who study not only the harvest but also the sowing of the seed. Humankind on Earth lives largely in a fog of mystery. But that which Is really is - and always will be. Therefore nothing has changed, because Reality is eternal.

If you would remember this you would not have to suffer the heartbreak to which the human soul is so frequently exposed.

We will leave you with three wise saws which may not strike you as modern instances but which we hope will serve to amuse as well as illuminate:

"He who standeth alone on one leg will not necessarily lose the use of the other."

"Hasten not to be slow, as delay is the natural outcome of hurry."

"Premeditated witty wickedness is not a deadly sin. Nay, more an amusing explosive quality which rids the soul, on its mortal level, of calculated maliciousness towards its challenging opponents.! "

2.8 Disease as Opportunity

Evenness of temperament is a highly desirable characteristic for health and well-being.

A healthy equanimity stems from a strong link with the true Self which is continually in a state of joy and peace, whatever the state of being of the personality. It is equally characteristic of maturity and grows with experience. In such a state both mental and physical being remain calm and objective in the changing circumstances of everyday life.

However, it must be remembered that on planet Earth the conditions are far from ideal. Emotions are part and parcel of conditions on any planet - although to varying extents - and are essential for the maintenance of health and well-being. On Earth this is even more true than it is elsewhere. Emotions act as an extremely useful outlet. By giving vent to anger or sadness or hilarity, much of the strain of life in incarnation is relieved, and the body, mind and emotions can return to a state of peace.

But where conditions are not ideal, emotions may become over-indulged or may be denied. Where normal emotional expression is denied and has no outlet, the powerful force of the emotion is then directed inwards. It does not disappear because it has been denied or suppressed but, turned inwards where it cannot have its normal release, it wreaks havoc on the individual's ability to be himself and to remain in a state of health.

Emotional denial is therefore not a once for all event. To prevent the denied emotion surfacing, denial must be maintained. This involves a great deal of energy. It also involves, at least at the extreme, a rigid control of behaviour and expression which kills any possibility of ease and enjoyment and spontaneity. Behaviour becomes stiff and ruled by habit, and the individual's ability to respond to inspiration is severely curtailed. Instead, he evolves rules and routines for maintaining control. Over time these become so much second nature that the individual is hardly aware of the regulations which govern his thoughts and his actions.

This is the basis of neurosis. Where the emotions are felt as more immediately threatening, where the fear in the individual is greater, neurosis shades into obsessive-compulsive behaviour - routines which start to take on a life of their own. The best known are compulsive hand-washing and anxiety about turning off appliances. In some the compulsion is so great that sufferers wash their hands raw or can barely leave the house for checking that the oven really is switched off.

Where control is less complete, more of the unacceptable emotion will escape. It will be seen in irritation, in tendencies to frustration over small matters and details. It also surfaces in something called projection. In this, aspects of the unwelcome emotion are seen in other people because it is too dangerous to face it in self. Thus, it is someone else who is aggressive or critical or judgmental or bad.

The other person may be none of these things. But where he has some resemblance to the person doing the projecting or, in other cases, someone important in that person's life who was critical or bad in the past, then he will "cop it" for something that has very little to do with him.

The power of the projection is so great, fuelled as it is by the immense power of the original emotional trauma which only increases in isolation, that the other person may even end up taking on the characteristics projected on him.

So where you have someone who was made to feel bad about himself at a crucial stage in his emotional development, and where badness was unacceptable, that person tends to project his unacceptable badness onto others - other classes, other races, for example. Or where an important adult in a child's life was felt to be hostile but the perception of hostility itself was unacceptable, hostility tends to colour the adult's relations with other people.

Cultures based on "sin" and lack of love, as are most cultures on planet Earth, frequently engage in mass projection onto other cultures. The alienation from Self felt by one person, one community or one nation is projected onto another person, community or nation, and gives rise to personal enmity, discrimination and war.

Emotions, as we have said, may also run out of control. Instead of being simply vents for the frustrations and difficulties of living they are given predominance over the natural checks and balances of a mature outlook. Emotional expression runs riot. In normal circumstances the release of anger lasts only a few seconds. But where the original trauma has not been resolved, anger can become an over-riding approach to life.

What kind of situations give rise to such powerful and dangerous reactions?

The situations of the greatest significance for all in incarnation are always to do with survival and identity.

In the human being, these are generally at their most powerful in the earliest part of life when the new personality is being formed.

The primary importance of the personality is that it is the means by which the Spirit can interact with the material world. Because of this, it must necessarily have a strong correspondence with the material through the physical being and the emotions. The concerns of the personality are survival and identity - and love.

The personality is formed both by the soul, with the learning and aims chosen for the incarnation, and by the circumstances of the new life, most crucially the nature and character of the parents and what is going on in their lives.

Nature, the reflection on the material level of Divine Law, ensures that these conditions are those ideally suited for the purpose.

It is easily seen in animals, for example, that most interesting creature, the cat. Just observe a cat - any cat. It washes itself, either sitting up or lying, in poses of hedonistic enjoyment, utterly absorbed in what it is doing. It is being itself with complete devotion, and enjoying itself thoroughly in the process. It does not stop being itself when frustrated, angry or sad. It enters into all its experiences with all of itself in ways which are individual to it. It welcomes its experiences and puts no barrier between itself and them.

But neither does the cat hang on to its experiences. Once one is done, it is always ready for the next one.

When kittens still in the womb become aware, they sense immediately this being Self and enjoying being Self in the mother and father cats. Both accept themselves as they are, and this acceptance, this enjoyment of Self and spontaneous being of Self surround the kittens with unconditional love. This is the only practical definition of love - simple acceptance of Self. From this alone flows acceptance and therefore love of others.

Feeling unconditional love all around them, the tiny new lives feel themselves to be loveable. Feeling loveable they love and accept themselves from the start. They identify with what they feel washing over them, with love, and thus with the true Self.

Accepting and loving themselves from the start they are born all prepared for the experiences and adventures and challenges that come with being a cat.

What is true of a cat is true of every other created being, including human beings.

When mother and father, or the important adults in the child's life, are accepting themselves and enjoying being themselves, the child will be born and grow up accepting and enjoying and loving itself. It will be full of self-esteem and self-confidence and eager for the experiences of life as a human being.

The loving state of the parents facilitates the bonding between parent and child. It is reinforced by touch and interaction - hugging, tickling, teasing and general enjoyment of the child by the parents. That allows the unrestricted bonding between the child's developing personality with its Source, the loving Spirit which animates the incarnation. Loving and accepting Self, the little self is at one with its true identity and is relaxed and at ease about being what it truly is. In such a state it cannot but be true to Self and open to the guidance of the Self in all it does.

This is wholeness, the basis of well-being and health.

Anything that disrupts this bond between the Spirit and the personality disrupts that easy, relaxed and joyful state of being. It ruptures the security felt by the individual in his togetherness with the true Self. It breaks the link, through the Self, with the Oneness in which all exist, whether or not they know it.

This can happen, even when the bond between personality and Spirit has been established. Wherever there are events involving trauma and fear, the bond can be shaken. Severe undermining can cause the individual to doubt himself and his inspiration. He can be thrown off course and then has to struggle to reassert his truth as best he can if he is not to go under.

Until he does, he may find that he develops various ailments which do not leave him until the Spirit is once more firmly in the saddle. There is a fine illustration of the relationship between the personality and the Spirit in the example of a horse and its rider.

Loving his horse, the rider - the Spirit - will take good care of it. Where horse and rider are in harmony, the journey proceeds successfully. The rider guides the horse along the best route to their shared goals and destinations, and the horse willingly bears the rider so that their joint purpose is achieved in a loving and enjoyable partnership.

However, where the horse, or personality, rebels against the rider, neither can go anywhere. The Spirit must wait until the horse calms down before he can get near it. Often he must stand well back until peace is restored. He will do everything he can to bring about the harmony which both horse and rider need.

Frequently the personality will have to experience difficulties and, on occasion, both shocks and judiciously applied encouragement to dislodge it from its rebellion and self-will. It may take many years, indeed, many life-times for a soul to run the gamut of its rebellion against its own higher Self. Its wayward course can encompass the extremes of negativity from self-destruction to destruction of others; from self-righteousness to complete anarchy; from utter passivity to the various extremes of power and negative interference in the affairs of other souls; from despair and loss to unrestrained greed.

All such experiences are nothing but opportunities - opportunities through which the soul can learn what is true and what is not.

The rebellious soul will attract to itself incarnations which give it the opportunity to come smack up against its rebellion. Thus souls burdened with, for example, guilt and self-destruction will incarnate into conditions which allow them to experience self-destruction to the full. Those full of hate and aggression will experience both hate and aggression and their opposites, persecution and suffering. Your planet has no lack of such conditions. You only have to look at the many oppressive regimes which brutalise the perpetrators as well as torture and kill their victims; or the regimes which encourage those who cheat, defraud and fail to provide for their people's well-being so that they end up poverty-ridden or starving; or those which, imbued with self-righteousness, burden their people with dogma and tread on their freedom to express and be and aspire so that none can aspire to the highest within them.

Many people on your planet seeing where the self-destructiveness in such souls takes them cry out against God : "How can He allow this to happen?", or worse: "How can there be a God when such things can be?" Foolish people, who cannot understand that in His great love the Eternal Spirit gives every soul the freedom it needs to come to its own understanding and realisation of who and what it truly is. Foolish ones indeed, who believe that being begins and ends with the body. The body is merely the reflection in the material of a glorious and shining original, the living Spirit in each and every one, which never dies, never suffers but exists in joy, peace and love. The erring soul, returning once more to its Source, bathes in its light; and in its love all the soul's temporary experiences in the world of matter fade like a dream at dawn.

Through its experiences the soul comes to a point where it has suffered enough to say: "No more." At that point it is as though a light comes on. The person looks at what he is doing and no longer likes it. Deep within himself he rejects it and begins to search for a better way. As soon as his inner orientation changes, life comes to help him. In fact, it is his own Spirit which shows him the opportunities which before, in his rebellion, he ignored. Gently, his Spirit leads him back to the path, and together horse and loving rider are able to resume their journey in mutual harmony and great satisfaction.

In all of this the greatest teacher is experience. As the rebellious soul draws to itself the consequences of its rebellion, it courts negativity in like measure to its degree of rebellion. There is nothing relaxing or enjoyable about destructiveness of self or others. There is nothing peaceful and life-enhancing in moralistic and critical attitudes. There is nothing constructive in weakness, fear or passivity. There is no wonder or joy in a life lived in resentment or envy or greed. The thrills of rebellion are those of anger characterised by adrenaline; they are purely material.

Eventually, even the soul most deeply immersed in negativity begins to realise that it is not really having a good time. It begins to realise that it is suffering. And when the soul has suffered enough, it is able to turn its gaze in a different direction; it begins to long for peace, for joy, for love. There may still be much ground to cover, but that longing turns the soul in the direction where its peace, its joy, its love truly lie.

The soul then has a great opportunity; to finally find out who and what it truly is; to begin to realise that it is itself the peace, the joy and the love for which it has been seeking.

2.9 Defences

Defences of various kinds are very necessary for the small child growing up in a loveless environment. Where one is weak and handicapped one needs crutches to help one walk. One needs something to drive one, to enable one to keep going in difficult circumstances.

Survival and continuity are therefore fuelled by anger for there is nothing else. Balance is maintained by various defence mechanisms. Thus a little one manages to cope with the world and its role in it as it grows up.

But growth is an integral part of human life and experience. Real growth requires that eventually the crutches be thrown away and that forward progress is fuelled not by anger, but by the natural and spontaneous creative potential of the Spirit.

If this cannot occur, what were once valuable aids become prison bars behind which the creative soul is penned and frustrated. What one depended upon to cope and carry one forward becomes an impediment to progress.

There are several stages of growing up in today's dysfunctional world as the soul struggles to regain its freedom and its joy despite the snares and tangles of negativity.

In this struggle, the greatest guide and help is joy. It passes through all prison bars, transcends all negative influences and aims true to its target, that of unfettered being as a creative and eternal Spirit.

30/9/97

2.10 Inner and Outer

Deep-seated feelings will one day be recognised as the prime movers of human action and human fate.

It is part of the dilemma of the human race on Earth at this time that it is almost oblivious to the part played in all that takes place on Earth by motivations, emotions and feelings, both within individuals and within groups of individuals. Thus, it attempts to attribute the causes of events and occurrences to other, quite spurious, factors, which although they may be concurrent are certainly not causal. For example, it is erroneous to talk of a gene for alcoholism, yet perfectly correct to note a gene which accompanies alcoholism.

For many ages the true moving forces of Earth's history have been ignored or suppressed. As a consequence history has repeated itself to the point where today it is rapidly grinding to a halt. For there has arisen a limited awareness of underlying causal factors in the human psyche, thanks to pioneering work by Freud, Jung and others. And more recently and more tellingly, people have been coming to a point of reckoning with themselves which has forced in many the necessity to look where they would not have dared to look before for a way out and a way forward: they have looked within themselves, and having looked there they have found that which humanity on this planet has ignored and reviled over the millennia - the peace and joy and love of the true Self; and they have stirred into being a new spirit in Earth's ages-old darkness.

Thus, *in extremis*, an aberrant situation is beginning to find its way back to truth as the blocks to knowledge and progress are discredited and start to be discarded.

We have spoken of these blocks before, but there is never any harm in repeating that which is true. For the blocks to knowledge and progress lie in all that causes the individual, or the group, or the nation, to look outside itself for the solutions it requires.

Thus there can never be peace in a country till there is peace in the hearts of the majority of its inhabitants. There can never be an end to an individual's persecution by others till that individual finds within himself the strength of his Spirit which gently washes away feelings of weakness and vulnerability, and against which his persecutors are powerless. There can never be an end to an individual's "bad luck" or failure or dissatisfaction with life till he identifies with the wisdom and guidance of the Spirit within. There can never be joy and direction and fulfilment in an individual's life until he embraces his own inner truth, his inner direction and the deep abiding joy of his true Self.

Viewed from the perspective of the Spirit, all earth life is but a dream. Each individual life is like a film produced and directed by the individual's state of being. It faithfully reflects what that individual is doing to himself, to his true Self. Frustrations,illness,delays, accidents, reversals, failures are all, as it were, the inner state writ large upon the stuff of outer events and people, messages for those who are open-minded to read and, if they wish, to act upon.

Are you in work which is causing you to become more and more tired and stressed? Do you feel dissatisfied with your situation in life and your prospects? Could it be that your true Self is trying to tell you that this work or this situation or some aspect of it is not for you? Or do you find yourself running around, always missing connections, expending your energies in achieving very little? What might this be saying about how truly your priorities reflect what you want to be doing in your innermost being?

Patricia, a lady driver, had a highly emotional experience in, of all places, a rather complicated car park building in Brighton. When she was ready to leave, she looked for her car without being able to find it. She searched for a long time without success and with increasing desperation until she realised she was looking in the wrong part of the building.

This lady was able to see how the situation mirrored the state of the tiny child within her which was still looking for the bonding she never had with mother and father. She was also able to see the humour of the situation and make a further step forward by laughing at the past.

These are simple, everyday examples. But they are also all opportunities, lovingly brought about by the true Self to help the personality to accept its love. In the main, this involves coming to terms with some aspect of very early experience, as in the example above. Less subtle but extremely effective opportunities are brought about by redundancy, the break-up of a marriage, illness, loss, and situations where an individual finds himself at a cross-roads, blocked at every turn in what he tries to do, or caught in a situation of great stress where he is unable to see a resolution. The more traumatic the situation, the greater the resistance in the personality to the ascendancy of its own Spirit.

These traumas can be shattering. But they are always preceded by far less shattering opportunities which have been ignored, starting with the kind of simple situation described above. Each time an opportunity is ignored, the Spirit will bring about a more compelling situation in its attempt to get through. If you find yourself in such an extreme situation, you will get nowhere by asking "Why me?" or blaming others or life or God. You yourself and only you yourself have brought this situation about.

And why have you brought it about? The answer lies on the level of your deepest aspirations which are to do with progress and wholeness. The Spirit will do whatever is necessary to bring into conscious awareness all that blocks unity with its vehicle. Thus, each such occurrence is nothing more than an opportunity to let go of attitudes, emotions, and conditioning which come between your true Self and its goal.

There is no need for dogma, or for genes, or for complicated training or health regimes or intellectual gymnastics. The truth is simple and straightforward. All welllbeing,all progress is a matter of Being - of being what you are - and all Being comes from the Spirit.

To achieve its fullest expression through its incarnation, the Spirit will undertake any and every experience possible to bring the personality into a realisation of who and what it truly is. For it is only by identification with the true Self that life can unfold in joy and progress and companionship and fulfilment.

A new era is indeed dawning. In it Earth humanity's deepest motivations will be increasingly the joy and fulfilment of the Spirit, and less and less the fear, rage and self-will which caused the blood-stained, repressive and destructive history of the past.

21/7/98

Chapter 3

Body

The natural state of being of man and woman and child, like that of the animals and the rest of Creation, is lightness and ease and lack of heavy, effortful thought.

We cannot stress enough the factors which are responsible for the present state of humanity on Earth. All the symptoms of physical and mental and spiritual disease have one cause and one cause only - the lack of identification with the true Self, or the refusal to identify with the Self, as it might also be viewed.

This we have discussed already and will discuss in greater detail later. But there are a number of related areas which also need to be taken into account.

The first concerns the physical body itself. As is now generally recognised on your planet, the world you inhabit today is polluted to levels which have far-reaching effects on the health of the body, and on the body's ability to nourish itself to the extent necessary for health and well-being.

As a result of these factors nutritional deficiencies, arising from the body's inability to synthesise or even extract what it needs from its nourishment, are now common. These affect energy and well-being. In sensitive individuals, they can even affect the emotional state, and will make it difficult if not impossible to function joyfully and at one with the Self.

To re-balance the physical being, supplements need to be taken. In your environment today there are certain food supplements which are exceedingly helpful for the maintenance of a good physical state:

1) A capsule of cod liver oil every day. Do not take it in liquid form from a bottle, please. You can overdose that way.

2) Bioflavanoids (citrus or anthocyanidin complex) for the benefit of your blood vessels

3) In European parts selenium, 200 mcgms daily, as the soil is deficient in this nutrient.

4) Last but not least, Co-Enzyme Q10, from 30 mcgms daily in your thirties and into your forties, then 60 mcgms until you are about 60 years old. After that, you can see if you derive more benefit by increasing to 100 mcgms. You will be surprised how young and vibrant you will remain! Your muscles, including the heart, simply require an adequate supply.

There are other helpful hints, but they are not for this kind of book as there are those who will not use them as directed.

Keeping the body well nourished and free from noxious poisons is the least you can do for your divine Selves.

No rider would knowingly get on a horse which was wrongly fed or had partaken of poisons such as alcohol, sugar, tobacco or caffeine-loaded coffee. He would know that the horse could not be controlled to his liking, and no-one could tell him otherwise.

If the horse were not fed adequately according to its nature, it would not have the strength and stamina and the calmness which the rider needs to perform his intentions.

3.1 Breathing

Deficiencies and nutritional poisons are still not the whole story as far as the physical body is concerned. The fear which earth humanity has embraced for so long has many ramifications, some of which this work attempts to describe. But one of the most immediately significant for the body is what fear does to breathing.

Natural breathing is slow and deep. The North American Indians, before they too fell from their oneness with all of Creation, breathed deep into the diaphragm, about three to five times per minute. "Fear breathing", as we may term it, is rapid and shallow so that the body does not get the oxygen needed, by the brain in particular, for best functioning. Breathing deep into the diaphragm ensures that the lungs fill with air so that an adequate exchange of oxygen and carbon dioxide can take place.

Where such breathing has not been practised, the diaphragm muscles will be weak and temporarily resist being made to work. They will need to be extended by particular effort. Natural breathing will feel unnatural to those accustomed to a life-time of "fear breathing" and it will take repeated efforts and mindfulness to change the habit.

We would like to point you to mindfulness in this particular case, although it is good practice in general to keep aware. Mindfulness will help you to realise when you are fear breathing so that you can correct it as soon as possible and thus quickly succeed in changing a useless habit.

Mindfulness will also help you to recognise when natural breathing reasserts itself. This happens particularly when you feel relaxed; you find yourself taking a deep breath in real contentment. The value of being aware at such moments is that it helps to give you the sense of what natural breathing feels like. It comes with relaxation and accompanies a feeling of peace and happiness. This state of being is not possible with fear breathing.

In other words, natural breathing is part of a state of being in which personality and Self are as one and at peace. Encouraging diaphragmatic breathing helps in the bringing about of this state as well as helping the brain to function as it should, as a receiving and transmitting station for thought and inspiration.

3.2 The Stress of Modern Relaxation!

It is not a natural or a healthy thing to subject the physical vehicle to excessive stresses when they are not necessary.

Yet such situations are a common part of what are called "leisure activities". So stressed and fearful have the developed nations become that they have evolved outlets for their emotions. The irony of such outlets is that through them the emotions are further wrung and emotional states exacerbated.

Sporting activities involving competition, which often lead to violence; theme parks with rides which are thought to be exciting but which have a highly stressful effect on the immune system; films and computer games involving thrills and violence which excite the stress system unnecessarily; loud violent "music" in which the beat actually acts on the heart to distort emotional responsiveness; ugliness and superficiality in art or entertainment which depress rather than uplift the state of being; these are some of the means of relaxing "chosen" by modern man in the so-called civilised parts of the world - and aspired to by those in developing areas! The humour of course escapes those who subject themselves to such stressful forms of "relaxation". But the effects of their chosen "leisure activity" on their physical vehicles, and especially on the immune system and the general emotional state, are very real.

Rather than providing an outlet for tensions, these pursuits actually contribute to an increase in the level of general anxiety. The heightened emotional state which modern man has been conditioned to view as happiness subsides to increased anxiety. Yet as anxiety and desperation lessen in you, you find that you become less and less able to tolerate this kind of entertainment or leisure activity; it becomes clear that it is a disturbance to your new-found peace and state of real relaxation. Then you can see, as we do, how such activities grow out of mankind's basic fear and rebellion. It will not then be difficult for you to act to protect yourselves against such forms of relaxation!

13/3/99

3.3 Stress Symptoms

Fear and apprehension are stress symptoms of your so-called modern civilisation. They are disturbing to the Spirit and produce negative thought waves of minor or major strength, according to the intensity of the state of fear.

It is of little avail to tell yourselves not to worry. Once such a negative conception has established itself in your thought pattern, no amount of contra-thinking will ever eradicate it from your subconscious mind. Every experience is there forever and cannot be removed by your physical brain-mind.

This is the cause of man's use of the innumerable "props" with which he seeks to dull his memory and perception. Tobacco, alcohol and a host of other drugs of all kinds are used in the mistaken idea that they would alleviate the emotional pain of the experience itself. But this is an error and man on Earth is only too used to making such blatant mistakes, precisely because he, so very often, fails to overcome the condition of terror within through the assertion of his spiritual maturity. Thus he commences to collapse before he has even attempted to assert himself, his real Self, his spiritual reality.

Fear and depression are not states of soul of mature spiritual man. On the contrary, their existence indicates that there is indeed much room for improvement. Nevertheless, one in such a state is not helped by attempting to force himself to discontinue his erroneous and lugubrious meditations on the material level, for this is a matter to which the Spirit alone can attend.

However, when man resorts to his potions or other escapes which he erroneously considers helpful, he does not only not allow the Spirit to manifest itself fully, but indeed actively hinders and prevents it from taking over the regime. Thus man falls back onto the lower strata of consciousness and existence, becoming increasingly irresponsible and rebellious towards his higher Self.

All you earthly people commit this omission. You come into the physical world to learn to comply with the requirements of the Spirit. Yet in your obstinate refusal to subordinate the personal exercise of free will to the demands of the Spirit for freedom to govern its earthly vehicle, you are obstructing the purpose for which you undertook incarnation.

3.4 Healing

Given that the lack of love of Self, arising from the schism between the Spirit and its incarnation, is the basic cause of all illness and disease, there is much which can be done by simple, spiritual healing.

Healing is the application of pure love. It is well-known and experimentally proved that certain doctors have a particularly beneficial effect upon their patients, and that this effect holds true no matter what treatment is administered.

Likewise, spiritual healers and faith healers often succeed where modern medicine fails because they are treating the patient with love rather than drugs. With love, complete cures can be and are achieved, even in the most difficult cases.

Patients can also help to bring about their own cure. Where their lives are out of kilter with the aims of the true Self, leading to strokes, heart attacks, cancers or other illnesses, patients can completely overcome their illness by recognising and changing their outlook and priorities in line with their true nature. Their illness becomes then a stepping-stone to greater fulfilment and enjoyment and achievement in a real sense.

It should not be forgotten however that, in the strange world that Earth humanity has fashioned for itself, there is also a place for medical and surgical intervention where nothing else will do.

19/11/98

3.5 Waste

Surpassing one another - in feats of body, mind or spirit - is a preoccupation which is happily and intensely pursued by human beings in physical incarnation on Earth. Indeed, you are indoctrinated with the necessity for competition, on the grounds that being one step farther ahead than the fellow next to you is a pre-requisite for "progress" in your world.

How can we explain to you the vacuum which this attitude creates between your brother's performance and your spurt to outdistance him? Between those two achievements lies a no-man's land which remains undiscovered and unused - a wasteland in which valuable released thought and effort run aimlessly amok between these two points.

Unused space of this kind is valuable ground squandered. The earth plane is littered with the results of the enormous wastage of human resources, which drastically disturbs the harmony of thought and action.

But this is only one aspect of gross waste which man, in his short-sightedness, allows himself to create. The example we have given is merely one of millions which arise through man's ignorance of spiritual and physical law.

3.6 Being Centred

It is extremely common on Earth to find individuals who are absent from their bodies, or who are not properly "in" their physical vehicle.

In this state, the body cannot co-operate with the Spirit to achieve their joint aims and enjoy the partnership. In fact, the body cannot feel good in such a state without the presence of its animating force.

There are a number of reasons why this state of affairs comes about. Many are "absent" simply because they have locked themselves so tightly into repetitive thought and mechanistic attitudes and behaviour that there is little room for the Spirit which then must needs stand back. These people are actually defending themselves against their own greater awareness in this way and, as a consequence, go through their lives like sleepwalkers, or automata, till something shocks them awake.

With others, the condition is not so ingrained. Many of you who are sensitives learn to escape from intolerable emotions such as fear in what is known as a "fugue", or flight from Self. This means that you are not properly in your own body and are therefore prey to the freely circulating polluted thought and emotion in your world until you allow your conscious awareness to re-connect with your physical vehicle.

The condition is unpleasant and even dangerous. It needs to be dealt with when it happens and avoided at all times. Apart from dealing with the origins of the fear, the best way to do this is to practice "centring" yourselves, or rather your awareness, in your own body. This is another aspect of "mindfulness" which we mentioned earlier. You can do it by constructing, with your mind, a protective layer, such as a cloak of protection or a transparent glass bubble, all around your physical being.

Once your cloak of protection or your protective bubble is in place, it will stop negativity from gaining a foothold in your consciousness. It will also act to make and keep you aware of being in yourself, being centred in yourself, or grounded - firmly anchored in your physical being which is just where the Spirit wants to be.

When you are centred in your own being, or grounded, not only are you protected from negativity, but you also identify more closely with the aims and aspirations of your inner reality.

In such a state you cannot help but feel strong, sure and on top of the world.

5/6/99

Chapter 4

Mind

4.1 Original Thought

Once upon a time there was no intellect as man lived through his understanding. Nor did he have to ponder his own thoughts as they were original and did not warrant analysis.

Progressive adulteration of creative original thinking resulted in the disturbance of man's capacity to withstand pollution, not only of physical creations but also of the totally passive and natural thought mechanism. The result of this kind of disturbing activity you can now recognise in the thinking patterns of modern man. No longer is original thought given free expression. Instead, it is seasoned with uncontrolled interference from lower frequencies which completely distort the originality and bring forth a hotchpotch of conceptions glibly spoken with great, also adulterated, conviction.

What, you may ask, could be done to return to the innocent state of truth? Let us give you an example of the easily detectable mixture of error and truth. Says she to him, "I love you more than my own life". Here we have a statement which has lost its originality and meaning through the spoken word. Can you find the error in this statement? Also, "It is my intention to become as perfect as possible".

To help man to receive and express unadulterated pure thought, one would have to advise him first of all to unite himself with his own Source, and in experiencing the role of transmitter or mediator of his own truth, to make the double effort of listening and speaking. That is to say he should express the words which he has received without the co-operation of the intellect.

Original thought is not a part of the everyday communication between mortal minds. It functions on the level of totality or wholeness, and expresses itself in conjunction with all the etheric organs of sensory perception. The entire being becomes a transmitter and every thought vibration is dealt with in the way of transmutation. Man's true progression will eventually lead to the knowledge and use of original thought, not only when he raises his consciousness but also automatically, at any given moment, when the Spirit takes over from the personality.

You must understand that the use of this mechanism cannot be learned but is man's reward for patient, forward-going activity.

Let us make you aware of the degradation which man has suffered because of his refusal to learn the not so mysterious but, rather, natural faculties which he possesses.

The dissolution of pure thought is the result of intentional pollution with the purpose of weakening man's resistance to the intentions of the forces of negativity. Mortal man's awareness is thus distracted and turned away from the eternal without his knowledge. His unity with his Spirit no longer exists and, like a fish out of its natural element, he struggles to find distractions which might serve as momentary sedatives to dull the conscience. It is not possible, however, to prevent feelings of guilt that cause irritations which transmit themselves through the mortal mind to the physical body. We have here the concerted effort of an intriguing and destructive force trying to drag humanity down to the point of no return.

We who are you and wish to help must communicate this situation to you so that you may be stimulated to think more clearly about it. This lies in your own hands and depends on your ability to turn stubbornness into humble recognition. The power of thought is very great and positivity expressed can never be destroyed. It has a life of its own which is eternal, and collectively it represents a defensive weapon which does not adhere to matter like your atom bombs, but is indestructibly useful.

4.2 Esoteric Thought

True esoteric thought takes place on a level of Oneness only. Any other so-called esoteric thinking has its origin in the intellect.

When a human being's soul has become a slave to its own intellectual powers and endeavours to grasp truth on that level, it is from the beginning condemned to distortion as it appertains to the physical faculties of man and has precious little to do with anything else. So we see man-kind clap-trapping in the use of occult conceptions or language and thus stimulating the physical emotional factors to such a degree that a euphoric state results

True joy expresses itself in silent adoration of Oneness and the wholeness of all Creation. It has an outward-going quality and is not concerned with personal feelings of well-being. True joy is always preceded by an act of service and takes pleasure in its results.

We who are you are at pains to watch over you and guide you in such a way that your own quality of perception becomes sensitive and functions in the way of the Spirit. It is, therefore, our mission to protect you from making the mistake of recognising a state of being as Reality when it is in itself doomed to failure.

4.3 Uncontrolled Thought

Man in his physical body on the physical Earth continues to go about his business of playing games of make-believe with himself and others. And there are no exceptions, because the further he has risen in his task of progression, the more he is inclined and tempted to flit from one state of consciousness to another. And since, on most occasions, he cannot control his spiritual movements on these flights of fancy, the consequence is that he gets himself into the most appalling messes.

We would urge all who are engaged in spiritual service to learn to control their thought, to consciously give consent to a change of direction and level instead of drifting bemusedly hither and thither in unconscious indirection. In such cases we then have to bear the clamourous complaints of many of those who work with us who loudly bewail their exhaustion. Indeed, some even think it is our fault, though we are the ones who bring them refreshment.

These states of exhaustion which come and go without any apparent reason or cause are simply the consequence of uncontrolled thought. This fact is not generally known to your world. And only a few have as yet come to realise the disease which this can cause to the physical man - or, as we should perhaps say in the days of the liberation of the women of your Earth, the physical person.

We would strongly advise you to set your aim at not more than three, or better still, two levels of thought. In this way you can manifest more strongly, more purposefully, and in more conscious focus. If you do this not only will you not dissipate your energies, but actually gain in health and strength and ease. Above all, you will be more useful channels for us who serve you as channels for your own Higher Consciousness.

In all that we tell you we are motivated by the desire to awaken man, to awaken woman, to awaken the human person to the reality which is his, which is hers, which is theirs; a Reality which, of course, is Spirit. The clear fact that these communications encourage you, dear reader, to think along these lines cannot have escaped your attention.

4.4 Avoid Self-analysis

May your souls escape human conflagration and may you always know the dividing line between the "I was" and the "I am"'so that you may remain on the right side of consciousness. May inner peace and calm be yours, in preference to agitation triggered off by mortal men and their negative vibrations. May you have trust in yourselves and not be misled into seeking recognition on the mortal level.

Once and for all accept yourselves as you are, then no longer concern yourselves with the feelings you have or the situations you are in, but simply accept them. A man who is always in need of asserting himself is indeed a poor creature - he has not yet found his divinity within himself, and no amount of knowledge will serve to bring him further in his progression.

Avoid self-analysis. It is a negative rather than a positive procedure. We warn strongly against the continuance of this practice, for the wrong analysis can create chaos within the consciousness. Better the humble wisdom of acknowledged ignorance than the arrogant folly of error parading as "wisdom". In far-away lands there are tribes which have not yet been touched by "modern civilisation". They rely solely and totally on their inner strength and guidance. Thus they manifest towards their environment from within, whilst the so-called civilised peoples of your Earth manifest from without towards their inner selves.

Can you not see that the latter process clutters up your inner being? And, when eventually this intake from without is again emitted, you are producing an indigestible mass of human thought, slightly mixed with that of your own, which will, of course, be completely unpalatable to those in your circle who receive it.

All that originates from within and is inspired thought must be of the highest, and those of you who are aspiring to progress would link up here; for at this level it produces emanations of pure thought and you can rest assured that it will have instructive and beneficial effects on all who listen.

Avoid taking in other people's thought emanations and keep yourself, as far as possible, a clear channel for your higher consciousness. The more simply you function in everyday life, the more suitable you become to receive pure communication.

We find the tendency - in the so-called civilised human being - towards continuous thinking, probing, studying, and even compulsive "meditation" to be a real hindrance. It leaves so very little space in your thought for us - so that we may find room to inspire.

4.5 Word Thinking

Mastery of the tendency to word thinking is a necessary step in the reduction of stress.

So many of you torture yourselves with excessive word thinking round old and well-worn grooves. It is all based on emotion, and the emotions arise mostly in the past. The result is that your level of anxiety increases; and with that your precious receiving and transmitting station, your brain, becomes so clogged up with stale thought and emotion that nothing from a higher level, which would bring you relief, can reach you.

Consider your way of life. How much do you take in of the thoughts and emotions of others through reading, through television and film, and through excessive intellectual activity in your dealings and discussions with others? How much of your thoughts are taken up with the doings of fictitious characters which feed into your own anxieties and concerns? How much does your thinking revolve around analysis of Self and ideas?

All such thinking simply feeds the emotionally-based word thinking and exacerbates it so that the peace you seek eludes you.

Yet you can assert yourself and defeat the word thinking very easily.

To do this it is important to limit the intake of emotional matter, except possibly that which is wholesome and positive, and intellectual matter, with the exception of factual material.

Then you simply need to speak to the word thinking as you would to, say, a naughty imp. Tell it that you will not stand for it, that it is going to have to go, and that you will keep on insisting that it does, no matter how many times you have to do so. Do not make a drama of this. Approach it in a spirit of gamesmanship and determination. If the attempt fails at first, just repeat it until you have eradicated the repetitive, wearisome thinking from your consciousness.

You can facilitate the procedure by encouraging your thinking to take place in pictures, which is closer to natural thinking. You will find that some word thinking still takes place. But as long as it is peaceful and reflective and has no adverse effect then you may allow this to occur with equanimity.

It is as well in this, as in all things, to bear in mind that you do not live in a perfect world. Rather than aiming for perfection, which places a heavy demand upon Self, we would encourage you to aim for lightness and ease and merriment.

Remember, however, that in the conditions on your planet, you must be continually vigilant. As long as you have emotional hangovers from the past that still require resolution, the word thinking will have a tendency to reappear when you least expect it. Thus, you must be prepared to repeat the procedure above until your Spirit is so firmly in the saddle that nothing can any more dislodge it or disturb your well-earned peace.

2/7/99

4.6 Unwelcome Thoughts

Most unwelcome thoughts have their origin in some form of disharmony in the being or soul of an individual. They arise from unresolved emotional material associated with difficult situations in the past.

For such thoughts to be overcome and peace to reign again serene, the original situation must be brought into the light of objective consciousness, that of the greater Self. There it has the opportunity to vent itself and simply melt and vanish in the loving truth of the Self. All such emotional hangovers are irritants which strive in this way to achieve resolution.

However, as long as the soul resists the light of its own truth and will not let go its hold on its distressing thoughts with their underlying emotions, continuing instead with the defences which have proved effective in the past, resolution cannot take place.

Only when the soul has matured to the point at which it is ready to take its first steps out of the increasingly uncomfortable cocoon of its defences can it begin to face the original trauma. In so doing, it sees it finally for the small thing it truly is in the greater reality of the Spirit.

In some cases, there is no alternative but to allow the free expression of the trauma in a safe and objective environment in which it will meet a loving but firm response. In this way the original emotions exhaust their force, having no further reason for being.

When the past is admitted into consciousness, it is dissipated simply by holding on to the consciousness of the true Self through all the means at the individual's disposal.

In truth, these disruptions from earlier times are like the effects of a breeze upon a pond - the water is ruffled and there is a minor disturbance, but the pond itself is unaffected. Once an individual knows his true Self and commits himself to it such events, though distressing, are but fleeting and cannot sustain themselves in the positivity of his being for there is nothing on which they can feed.

They are, to put it another way, a necessary evil which allows unexpressed material from the past to emerge from its secret places in the subconscious. As long as this material stays there, it acts to drain the personality of confidence and energy or, worse, to feed on negative attitudes, emotions and motivations. Emerging into the radiance of the true Self, it is gradually dissipated and becomes no more.

Without this unpleasant but necessary process, further progress could not take place. It is important to prepare the ground, to break up all the obstructions to progress so that proper foundations for the soul's enterprise in incarnation can be laid.

In this way, the past is gradually voided of its power and the present comes into its own and reigns supreme.

4.7 Simplicity

It is wisdom to permit a conception of simplicity to take precedence over the complex functioning of the so-called civilised human brain. Simply stand within the stillness of eternal peace. Breathe in the life-giving and cleansing force of serenity.

Take time off from doing and thinking in a complicated manner based on your hard-won learning. Give yourself over completely to your pattern of life. Do this with your spiritual senses rather than with your feelings. Acquire that total state of receptivity which is the foundation for complete relaxation. Learn to recognise yourself as a perfect part of the great All there is and give your thoughts the holiday they deserve.

Consciously rise in stature above all that which is of the mortal world so that you can live in complete harmony and remain fundamentally unperturbed by its disharmony, pollution and turmoil - standing out as one who is in, though not of, that world. This is essential for all spiritual servers because the many souls who depend on you for help, knowledge and guidance, cannot see weakness as an example.

Remember that man in human incarnation is not what he appears to be. Therefore you must learn to put your trust in others without becoming emotionally dependent upon them. Trust is only misplaced when you are so involved that the emotions take control. Always ensure that the mastery remains securely in the hands of your own Spirit.

Just as you, as a person, are being encouraged to find your at-one-ness with your higher Self, so this need is also awaiting fulfilment in your world, the nations and peoples of your world, and in its communities and organisations.

Each community, or organisation or nation, has its own spiritual level of consciousness which is the sum total of the individual awareness of its members. The radiation of these frequencies is sensed by the unenlightened as well as the enlightened, that is to say, those whose aim is to further the truth of the All there is. The further progressed a people is in its understanding that the Law of Cause and Effect operates in all circumstances, the wiser and greater will the communal spirit become. And just as a truly contented community spirit emanates peace and love, so will it also produce a warming, welcoming and helpful response to the newcomer.

Chapter 5

Emotions

Erring thoughts lead into all kinds of tangled thickets and down distracting byways. It can be an interesting exercise to view the human consciousness in terms of a landscape. This landscape varies in beauty, in harmony and in "wholeness" according to the pre-occupations of the individual consciousness. Some landscapes can be downright hair-raising. Others are dreams of order and loveliness and peace. Most contain a wide variety of terrain, but where there is a oneness with Self and a commitment to truth, a broad straight path may be discerned. There may be vegetation which strays on to the path: sometimes branches grow across it, seeming to obstruct the way forward; but the path remains, straight and true to its goal, and all obstructions give way in the end before its strength of purpose.

This is only rarely found in human consciousness on Earth today. Most people's consciousness has no real focus. Most have indeed very little awareness; their thoughts circle round in well-worn grooves which may be seen as paths going nowhere. They are kept in their mazes by underlying, often extremely powerful, emotions. To stray out of the groove means confronting these emotions head-on. For most people, this is too frightening to contemplate. Fear, which is one of the powerful emotions, keeps them penned in and their lives remain safe but stagnant.

Sooner or later the emotions, denied an outlet, will attack wherever there is a chink in the defences against them. If they can find no way past the ramparts of repression, suppression or whatever defence is used, they will either manifest in the outside world through the individual's interaction with events and people, or they will attack the physical being.

To get back to our landscape: if you can imagine its huge extent, reflecting the vastness of consciousness, and if you can see the individual awareness crammed into a tiny part of the entire available scenery, then you can understand the complete mismatch between the potential of the individual and what that individual is doing with it.

Fear is not easy to confront; neither are anger and rebellion, nor the ever-present guilt feelings carried *ad infinitum* by so much of earth humanity. Yet were the individual to make that seemingly huge step outside his cracked-record thinking and face up to what is keeping him imprisoned, he would find that it is not so frightening as he thought. He would find that, in stepping beyond his self-imposed limits, a new road starts to open up to him.

Once upon that road, he would then quickly come across a whole vast and wonderful world he never suspected could exist. It lies there, just beyond the fear thoughts, the guilt feelings, the rage; it is just a little past the despair, the loneliness and all the other manifestations of the personality - a personality which has been traumatised by the world which formed it, and which then fears and hits out at that world and at its own loving Spirit.

Were the individual indeed to take his courage in both hands and confront all that limits and imprisons him in his endless grooves and discard it, he would find himself breathing a new air, the air of freedom to be what he actually is.

This new air is heady for those imprisoned long and deep in their mistaken sense of who they are. It may take some time to adapt to it, but love of Self eases the transition.

In fact, only love of Self can bring about the freedom of a captive soul. Only love can overcome the power of fear and the destructiveness of the negative emotions which trap and imprison a soul. Love of Self is the key to unlock the door; it is the key to a new life, lived at one with Self.

15/9/98

5.1 Laughter and Tears

The fringe benefits of spiritual thought are by no means to be scoffed at, for they are like raindrops which fall on the periphery - and they will, in direct proportion to the density of their fall, act as stimulants to man's thinking.

This process is similar to that which homeopathic medicine sets up in the physical body of man on Earth. Just as these remedies encourage the anti-bodies to resist and fight a particular disease, so would the minute particles of spiritual thought incite man to think.

Eventually, however, man has to decide whether he would prefer to remain in a stationary condition, satisfied with his small portion of heavenly breath, or whether it would seem desirable for him to lift his thought to a higher frequency and receive enlightenment - which may come, on occasion, even by way of a shock treatment.

Whichever choice you would make the end result would eventually be Oneness. In the first case the time factor may well be considerable. In the second, it would enable you to take your examination of maturity at an early date, thus leaving yourself prepared and open for further rapid progress and development.

You may well ask the question why progress is necessary. And our answer will be to invite you to use your imagination. See yourself remaining at a given point of understanding and see the results of your spiritual activity - stagnation. And hence, through the frustration it breeds, you will incur the lack of all those things which otherwise would be, according to spiritual law, "added unto you". Then see the eventual disease in your physical body, mind and emotions.

But we will now talk to you about the inner emotional core or seat of the emotions. As Spirit in a vehicle which is called physical body, you must needs be subjected to conditions and reverberations which operate in terms of a material or physical

level of understanding.
The soul is not always able to conquer the emotions which strongly upsurge in order to manifest - and consequently escape from the original site of their activity. Here then we see a state of conflict between Spirit and matter; and it is law that matter should be permitted to surface, so as to give Spirit space and room to function. All attempts to prevent the upsurge of emotion are a denial of the natural consequences: the healthy outburst of joyous laughter, the sobbing release of tears and so forth.

Here it is that those who have been brought up from childhood to keep a "stiff upper lip" fail to promote the Spirit's right to conquer and manifest cleanly in everyday life and experiences.

We would beg all humanity to question deeply the reason for man's ability to laugh and cry; and to see, in these two faculties, a wise provision which should be neither shunned nor despised. In giving vent or expression to these very creative gifts, man will eventually work himself into a state of peace and calm - the true outcome of the attainment of the oneness with his true Self.

Man's super-imposed urge to deny these two faculties, laughter and tears, is a stumbling-block in his own progression. Moreover, we would appeal to all parents, educationalists and those in loco parentis to let a child have free play in the expression of its emotional feelings. This also applies to men and women in their adult state.

Just as the fluid called tears contains a cleansing agent which affects the eyes in a positive manner, so the shedding of tears purifies the soul. Indeed, the ability to weep and to laugh freely will and must and does set man free - at least for a certain time - from his own inhibitions.

Through this very real process of cleansing man will, at the precise time of the incident, achieve a clearer vision of his problems and of the right way to overcome them.

5.2 Fear

The soul has its reasons for incarnating into a specific set of circumstances; but once it has entered them, it quickly forgets and simply reacts to what is going on around it. It is then in a state of great receptivity, needing love and harmony in order to remain at peace.

This inner peace is possible only when there is freedom from fear.

Fear, by its very nature, causes identification with matter as it is perceived by man on planet Earth. That means matter is accepted as a reality rather than the three-dimensional image it actually is.

The disharmony, the hostilities, the anger and the hates of the key figures in the environment invariably shock the child, whether already born or still in the womb, into a state of hypnosis. In this state, the thoughts and feelings given verbal or unspoken expression by these persons become hypnotic suggestions or engrams planted in the subconscious mind of the child. They may stay there for its lifetime, colouring all its activities, or the lack of them, affecting its relationships with other people, the world at large, and most of all its own self-image.

To reduce the fear, the little one adopts all kinds of "security blankets", mental, physical, emotional or behavioural, with which it then identifies. These act as anchors, something to hang on to, to and provide a sense of security when identification with the true Self has been undermined.

Letting go of fear is then the great difficulty. It is like stepping into the void. In a state of fear, the adult is locked into infantilism which finds freedom threatening as it means self-determination and decision-making. Freedom means standing on one's own two feet and taking chances, daring to be Self come what may. It can also mean standing alone and being different which is completely at odds with the inner, terrified child.

In a perfect world the good feeling about Self which stems from the ultimate reality of the soul would be nurtured and supported and encouraged in full measure by equally wholesome adults in a wholesome society. This would lead to an uncompromised creativity corresponding to the maturity of the soul itself. In creation lies joyful fulfilment of both playfulness and purpose. Fun, laughter and enjoyment are part of the soul and in themselves, therefore, creative. Deadly seriousness is a sham and looks exceedingly funny from the level of true reality, like a clown with the corners of his mouth painted downward.

The whole Universe is dancing to its own music, and man must learn again to enjoy himself with it. He must and can find his way out of his post-traumatic stress disorder, out of feeling vulnerable, fearful and angry, and start to realise his essential immortality in the magnificence of the true scheme of things.

5.3 The Release of Fear

Fear is the twilight of your two states of consciousness. Living in fear is experienced both in the mortal and also in the spiritual state of awareness. It is originated within the sum total of your experience on the mortal and on the spiritual plane. It is a very necessary release which encourages and demands progressive thought each time it occurs.

The release of fear removes fragments of negative thought which have been absorbed through the senses together with positive thought. This process of stimulation, through anxiety or fear, persists during your life on Earth. It is not to be shunned but rather to be welcomed. This does not apply only to man but also to nations, as well as to the Earth plane as a whole.

Each time you work your way through the valley of apprehension, you emerge a stronger and wiser person. While you are undergoing this experience you may suffer emotionally, but the eventual release from this tension, brought about through, once again, raising your consciousness a little higher, will give you a feeling of achievement and joy.

Fear is a driving force which leads in the end to the cleansing of matter and Spirit - a process which is essentially the cleansing of thought. You may take an example from the nations of your Earth who periodically drive each other into frenzied states of fear, with its concomitant expression of aggression, greed, envy and so forth. Ultimately the outcome of this release of fear would be either war or greater peace. Whichever one of these choices is made, there will arrive, after a time of suffering and uncertainty, a more cleansed state of being.

Therefore accept fear as a very necessary condition - and stop fearing fear!

5.4 Desperation, Anger, Despair and Depression

Desperation must be seen as, at best, a poor guide in dealing with the complexities of life. At worst, it will lead a soul altogether off its appointed path and down highways and byways that have little to do with the well-being of the body, mind or Spirit.

Desperation is an emotional state. It is compounded of fear and frustration. So intense is it that it cannot easily be suppressed and will act therefore to drive one so afflicted to be continually doing - attempting to distract himself through constant over-activity. When he cannot sit and do nothing, when he has to be continually "on the go", when he is driven by ambition or fear into overwork, or by anxiety into, say, excessive sports or shopping, desperation lies behind the drive. When he finds himself on a short fuse, when he needs constant new experiences or thrills to keep from being bored, the chief reason is desperation.

Desperation is entirely rooted in the material level. It has nothing to do with the Spirit. In such a state the sufferer cannot easily relax or find peace, for as soon as there are no distractions the underlying emotions, which are so near the surface, make themselves felt.

Much of the culture and "accepted wisdom" of this planet has evolved to deny or deflect the impact of the very real and terrifying feelings underlying desperation and, indeed, all aberrant emotional states. They are feelings of weakness and vulnerability, powerlessness and stark fear, and rage and frustration. Some of these feelings are almost impossible to tolerate, so intense and overwhelming are they, especially to a sensitive. The small child will do anything it can to reduce the impact.

The most accessible outlet for such feelings is anger. Anger is part of the life-force. It is an assertion of Self. Where the new incarnation is experiencing mortal fear, anger is a life-saver. It carries the little one through; it gives him something to hold on to. It provides a necessary expression for his feelings about his situation, especially his fear.

Where the little one cannot call on anger, all too often it finds its situation - in particular, its fear - so overwhelming that it cannot but let go of the body. This is a major cause of still-births and premature deaths of infants. Among the many aspects of human nature that your world does not fully recognise is the deadly nature of fear. Fear is a killer, and is the root cause of many otherwise mysterious early deaths. It must be said that it is not the only one. On occasions a soul will choose to leave the incarnation at this early stage in order to help its parents or other important individuals in the environment to learn something through the experience. Sometimes both reasons govern the situation, for the Spirit is adept at, as you would say, "killing two birds with one stone" so that the Divine Plan can unfold as it must.

But where there is anger carried over from earlier incarnations, then that anger can be the saving of the new life in its sore oppression. Only anger is powerful enough to counteract the deadly effects of fear. However, further problems arise, depending on the culture. There are many societies on your planet in which the direct expression of anger is unacceptable. The new life must then suppress this too.

Where anger is accepted and understood the little one can in turn accept and express and thus rapidly let go of his feelings, almost as soon as they arise, with consequent relief and the restoration of calm and harmony. Where anger is not accepted and has to be suppressed, there is no possibility of relief. The suppressed rage, penned in its prison in the subconscious, merely accumulates with further experience. Those of you who have experienced the force of infantile rage, in yourself or others or who have seen it in the infant, know how powerful it is.

This is the motive force behind lives given over to violence and destruction. It lies behind criminality and terrorism and much war-making. Thus it can be seen that the little one whose anger is unacceptable to the adults around him has a huge task to try to contain his rage. He learns to fear his anger, and with his anger, himself, for the anger is himself.

It may be helpful to reflect that anger, whether conscious, subconscious or unconscious, is in its last analysis always derived from an injury to the soul itself. This is the only way in which the kind of treatment of little ones described can be seen. There is no-one who can be blamed. It passes down the generations of traumatised infants who become traumatised adults.

For, always, behind the anger lies the fear. Fear and anger always go together. Excessive rage, temper, irritation and frustration always arise from deep, unresolved fear. Where these facts are not understood in the case of the baby and the toddler, and where there is also the longing for love which is continually frustrated, the result is more than likely to be states of desperation or despair.

In more extreme cases, where outlets for real creativity and assertion in later life are lacking, you find the life-denying condition of depression.

The experience for the sufferer is extremely unpleasant. It takes a great deal for him to be able to find the strength to assert his authority over the feelings these emotions bring about in him.

Yet it can be done. The feelings themselves need to be tracked down to their origins so that they can be released. This is possible with wise and mature assistance, although there are old souls who manage to accomplish a great deal for themselves. Much can be achieved by the victim simply by stopping the behaviour to which the underlying emotions are driving him and facing what he would rather not face. In doing this, he is already reaching for his own Reality, for its strength, its determination, and its love, which is the only way that the pull of the material can be overcome.

For it is only the Spirit which can heal the pain. Those who have been identifying with their desperation and despair and the emotions which give rise to them have been seeking their sense of themselves in what is not real. This they quickly realise as they are able to let go of the old emotions and identify with the reality of the true Self. In the light of that supreme objectivity, the insubstantiality of the unloving past which has been governing their lives for so long becomes unmistakable.

Understanding and thus resolving these emotions can only take place when the soul is ready to let go its burden.But there is another difficulty which may also need to be resolved.This is the tendency to project the unloving parent onto not only other people but onto the Spirit itself.The way out of the mess is through the love of the Greater Self.But if the Greater Self is mistakenly seenasparent-anxious,demanding,controlling, interfering,critical,undermining, unreliable or even aggressive - then the way out is barred, and the projection itself needs to be de-programmed.

The expertise of souls of great inner maturity who have already fought the battle and who are working with their own reality helps the process immeasurably.

The condition of despair differs from desperation in that it tends to be more passive. Yet it cannot either be viewed as normal or healthy - except in one sole aspect: when it can be used as an impetus to change by a soul prepared to let go of the past.

This situation is recognised in human culture in the saying: "When you hit bottom the only way is up".

Despair can, at this extreme, unlock the fighting spirit which at all other stages of despair is notably absent. It is the fighting spirit which is often the only way out of despair and depression and other such debilitating conditions. Indeed, such conditions arise when the fighting spirit in the sufferer has been repressed or suppressed and turns inward.

For the fighting spirit to be unlocked and the paralysis to end, there has to be a recognition in the sufferer that there is no-one else he can blame, no-one else to whom he can look to deal with the situation, no-one else who can make his effort for him except himself alone.

The way out of despair is a step into a more mature outlook, a step from passivity into true activation. It highlights the fact that this is fundamentally an infantile condition. In it, both the vulnerability and the powerlessness of the infant dominate the consciousness of the adult, accompanied by the infant's frustration and anger at its powerlessness to change the situation which is causing it so much distress.

When that anger is unable to find an outward and constructive expression in assertive or creative action, it turns inward and rampages against the Self in all its fury. The result can range from passivity to hopelessness to self-sabotage, self-sacrifice, even self-destruction. It is little wonder that the sufferer sometimes fears he is losing his mind, because an individual divided against himself cannot function in any positive or constructive manner.

In despair there is suppressed anger and rebellion and hopelessness. This is a potent mixture in the psychic atmosphere of the planet. Despair and desperation lead to the breaking down of limits. They say "So what? There is no God (i.e. loving parent) anyway, so what does anything matter?" A deprived humanity projects its anger and despair on the Eternal, the Creator of all. Father (or Mother) God is accused of not caring. Rebellion and cynicism hold sway.

It is a different matter when a truly creative outlet for the anger is found. The sufferer may still be racked by the trauma of the original situation, but life becomes worthwhile through the ability to act, to create, to produce. How many of the great souls throughout history suffered from deep personal difficulties yet were able to allow their genius, their true Self to contribute its creativity or its leadership or its inventiveness to the world! They are examples of real commitment to the true Self. Such a commitment cannot be forced; it is either there in the soul or it is not. When it is, it over-rides the traumatised personality and blazes a light for the traumatised everywhere in every time.

Where despair has not yet achieved full mastery of a heart, the individual is also prey to hope. We say "prey" for this hope is that of the despairing little one, desperate for its parents' unconditional love, desperate for their acceptance, their recognition, their understanding, desperate to feel it is loveable. Such hope can become a manic, overpowering force. It is doomed to be dashed; firstly by the reality of the original childhood situation in which the important adults were incapable of giving the child what it needed; and, later, by the failure of the adult world to heal the infant's wounds no matter how hard it tries, for by this age the infants concerns are quite inappropriate, being of the past.

Only the Spirit within can, at the adult stage, change the downward spiral. And only when the soul itself is weary of its seesaw between hope and despair or, where hope is absent, of the unrelieved heaviness of pure depression, only then is there a chance which can be seized to turn things in another direction.

The turnaround can be greatly facilitated and accelerated by spiritual psychotherapy where the soul is ready. It supports and encourages the wakening positivity by clarifying the situation and confirming the new direction. Only one who has himself experienced such a turnaround can be of real assistance to another in the same situation, and only a born spiritual psychotherapist can successfully guide another soul into the light of its true reality.

We make these points at a time when light is reaching into the darkest and most hidden places in the layers of consciousness around planet Earth and forcing what lurks there out into the open. For as it touches places of the very deepest despair and hopelessness, it causes the suffering souls to look up out of their darkness and become aware of a way out, a way of real, not imagined, hope.

There is always a way out. But not everyone is willing to take it. Some cling to their suffering because their anger and resentment are so great that they do not wish to absolve those who caused it or who, they believe, contributed to it, by letting go and leaving it behind.

Such resentment is a very great danger. It creates an environment in which a soul cannot thrive, but must at some point cause harm to itself or to others. A soul which nurtures resentment cannot be true to Self and will not recognise the Self either in itself or in others. There is nothing the Spirit can do with such obduracy. And when it is fuelled by fear, as is usually the case, the resulting negativity can spread its black stain over many long decades, even over centuries.

This is what is happening and has been happening for hundreds of years in the Balkans and other dark areas on the globe. But it also happens on an individual level in every nation and everywhere there are human beings on planet Earth.

All it takes to resolve the situation is to let go, as has happened to a significant extent in, for example, Northern Ireland. But letting go of such deep negativity requires a real leap of faith backed by an act of will. On a national level these efforts can only be taken where there is a coming together of both sides under an uncompromised, wise and loving leadership, even if it starts with only one small step towards the other. On an individual level, letting go must be facilitated by an understanding of the situation of the soul.

What is the situation of the soul? Why, nothing more than its repeated forays into incarnation upon the Earth, forays in which it has been, at different times, both victim and aggressor, both foolish and wise, both leader and follower, both positive and negative, both male and female, and so on. For the adventures of the soul in incarnation have only one aim: knowledge of its true nature whilst in incarnation so that the incarnation may become a vehicle for the shining glory and the multi-faceted talents of the eternal Spirit which animates it.

In pursuit of this aim, the soul undertakes many different lives which are in actuality many different learning situations. Through its experiences it begins to discern the eternal truths which are the majestic - although mainly ignored - backdrop to the doings of Earth humanity. And as it builds up a deeper insight into the real truth of life on Earth, it comes to know more and more the truth of its own nature as an eternal Spirit. Where the soul knows its own truth, the challenge of life on Earth is to hold on to that truth and live by it and let it shine in the midst of the untruth which surrounds it.

And where the soul has found its positivity and the means by which it can maintain it, it has found home. In deep contentment and shining joy it pursues its appointed path towards its fulfilment in utter co-operation with life, with all of Creation, knowing itself as part and parcel of the great Oneness which is the Universe.

28/7/98

5.5 Guilt Feelings

Sin is a human invention. Most often it is applied to the infraction of some man-made rule or regulation, or simply to the failure to conform with the accepted norm.

Rulers and religious leaders have seen fit for thousands of years to foster feelings of guilt and fear of punishment in their populations. The power of these overlords depends on the submission of their subjects to an intricate network of convoluted, iron-clad rules or laws or dogma.

The idea of "sin" carries with it a rigid judgement, and judgement means guilt. The psyche burdened by feelings of guilt expects punishment. Punishment is only one step removed from penance which, after all, is nothing but self-imposed punishment.

Guilt feelings in the soul often express either in some evident form of masochism, or in aches, pains, disabilities or disease, all indicating the dis-ease in the soul with its uncomfortable load. Cultures preoccupied with "sin" generally shame children for their perceived misdeeds which are often simply infractions of the accepted and demanded dogmatic norm. An indoctrinated sense of guilt and shame precludes free and creative expression of Self, substituting conformity for diversity.

Being shamed repeatedly by the important adults in a child's life leads to self-consciousness which, by its nature, is fear, the fear of disapproval and loss of love.

5.6 The Mirror - A Case History

All eyes at this time are focused upon an apparent trial in the United States. But the real trial is already well advanced and now approaches its final - not judgement - but rather d'enouement.

For in reality it was never the President of this great country who was on trial. In the annals of eternity, the temporary values of a temporary society leave little trace. Only the great truths engrave themselves for all time and all places. That you may know them, we set them out: they are the truth which is being true to Self; love and compassion; peace and unity; joy and strength;creative endeavor;and progress.

On these counts, the President cannot help but pass with flying colours. This is an exceptional soul who has given great service to the world. Even in this present instance he is serving the cause of the eternal and the Divine. How is he doing this? He is acting as a lightning rod, as it were, to conduct the release of a great negativity from its dark lairs where it feeds on human hearts and drains them of love, of compassion and of truth itself.

What he is doing can also be understood as holding up a mirror to his people, indeed the people of the world, in which they can see themselves, as much victims of the culture of "sin" as he himself.

In speaking of the great negativity, we refer to the one and only "sin"there has ever been, which is that of the concept of "sin" itself. We use the Earth word "sin" but we would rather label it a disharmony which sets itself up in opposition to the all-pervading harmony of the Divine. Or it could be viewed as a lack of love in the face of the infinite love of the Divine, or a petty war conducted by the ego, or temporary self, against the peace of eternity.

The pernicious nature of this disharmony has been understood by the truly great souls among you. One of these, Hildegard of Bingen, called it by its name and refused to have any truck with the concept of "sin". Another, John Milton, set down the means by which rules to condemn "sin" and enforce "virtue" are seen as inimical to true virtue itself, which can only be embraced within each and every soul of that soul's own volition.

But the world has gone its way ignoring the words of the wise. In truth, the concepts of "sin" and "virtue" and "morality" have proved too richly rewarding for all those whose level of striving concerns itself with personal gain and power. Multitudes have profited from the concept of sin. Multitudes have achieved what they never deserved through talent or effort or commitment to their own inspiration, thanks to "sin" and "ethics" and "morals".

These concepts lie at the heart of the greatest negativity like a nest of vipers, and it is this negativity which the true soul in America is helping to bring out from its hiding places and into the light of day for all to see.

No, it is not the President of the United States who is on trial. He only holds the mirror in which can be seen the trauma which afflicts nearly all on this traumatised planet. Who then can judge one who is simply their own reflection?

The real trial is of every human heart around the globe. In this great scales of a greater justice than that of poor, flawed human institutions each heart is weighed, not to be judged by others but that it may know itself. It is being weighed for the love in it, for the joy it contains, for the truth by which it abides.

On Earth there are many truths, most of them spurious. It is the business of each soul to weigh them and judge them by their degree of harmony with the indwelling Spirit, and by their consequences. Thus a soul learns and grows in wisdom, though in all too many cases that growth will be long yet in coming. Only the truth which is eternal can answer the soul's longing and bring it joy and help it fulfil its purposes. The truths of Earth can never do this.

The rules and standards of Earth can only add to the trauma afflicting the planet as they have done down the ages; they imprison the longing soul and bring it pain. And those on Earth who have instituted and maintained and perpetuated these rules and standards and judgements over the long years will find that they fly back in their faces, pressing for recognition through the pain of a dawning understanding of the truth of the eternal.

Let it be clearly understood: the concept of sin arises directly out of earthkind's rebellion against the loving God, the Creator Who is present in all things, in all souls, in all Creation. When humans on Earth turned away from the Self, the Divine in each one, they turned away from truth, from joy, from love, from peace, and from the harmony and unity of all Creation. Ever since they have been staring into the abyss.

Now the abyss has become a mirror in which all have the opportunity to stare their rebellion in the face and recognise it for what it is. Thus they may free themselves, should they wish, to turn again to their inner truth which is the only truth. They can reclaim their identity with that truth and open the door they had closed to universal joy and harmony and love.

This process of recognition is the truth of all that occurs on Earth at this time. In this process, a great influx of light from the heart of Creation is driving negativity out into the open, to be seen at last for what it is, without disguise, without its thousand and one tricks which it used to fool those who were willing into its snares. Now all must know what is truth and what is not, and all must choose. This is the healing opportunity for all who have endured Earth's sordid story down through the millennia, and who wish to be part of the new world which is coming into being.

So how will America choose? How will the world choose? We would say to you only that negativity has had its day, and that a new world beckons and a new life awaits.

But the vipers have a lot of hissing still to do, and all the poison must be extracted for the new world to be able to come into its own.

20/9/98

5.7 Peace

Obstinacy, self-will, anger, rebellion and guilt and many more have their place in the head. They try to feed, as thoughts, on the Spirit and quite often succeed in diminishing its vitality. Spirit, temporarily deprived, seeks to inform the heart of its precarious situation.

The heart responds with an increase in its beat and consequent palpitation.

Do you wonder then, that the knowing man who has found the way to inner balance through his own humility, through the surrender of the emotions and the personality to the true Self, rejoices in the newly-acquired state of peace and joy? No longer does exaltation animate his emotions. Nay, on the contrary: his acquiescent, non-aggressive, peaceful state of being restores the Spirit's equilibrium. At once the personality will be called to order and it retreats into the consciousness of the One.

5.8 The Tyranny of Perfection

Dear ones, in the vicissitudes of life in incarnation we would beg you to beware the tyranny of perfection.

Remember that your world has been and is in the grip of an ages-old aberration which today is recognised as post-traumatic stress disorder. But what today's experts do not recognise is that this affliction is not limited to those who have been in wars and atrocities and accidents. Its symptoms are borne by nearly all in incarnation, for all have suffered the even greater trauma of being born into a world without love, without the loving acceptance and understanding and recognition which is the right and need of every new life.

The consequences of this mean that all, from the highest to the lowest, grow up with a gross deficit, physically, emotionally, mentally and, most of all, spiritually. Without the unconditional love of the parents or important adults, the child cannot love or accept its own Self. Its life is then traumatised and scarred until it finds a way to resolve this dilemma.

There are those who, despite their appalling deficit, remained true to Self and to its aims and creativity. They were not understood by their peers; they were even reviled; but their legacy survives down the ages. Great artists, writers, scientists and philosophers, leaders and explorers and businessmen who transformed the world - they are to be lauded, especially when they were at the same time all too human.

In the great light of truth what counts is not whether such souls measured up to the inconstant and generally petty criteria of particular cultures and particular times. On the level of objectivity, even such a one as Mao Ze Dong was good for humanity on balance, for despite his many actions against his own people, he set free the women of his country to pursue their own destiny in a major act of enlightenment.

More than this cannot be expected of any in incarnation on planet Earth. So, dear ones, when it comes to yourself and others do not expect perfection. Especially do not demand it, in either others or yourself. For where you are following your inner light and bending your efforts to achieving your inner aims, then much in the way of faults and failings - even those the world in its vanity and moralising believes to matter - simply pale into insignificance in the glory of that achievement in these conditions.

5.9 Demands

Demands of any kind are inimical to simple being. Making demands on another person, or accepting the demands of another, instantly makes natural being impossible.

The flow of being, characterised by spontaneity, ease, inspiration and joy, is shattered by the making and accepting of demands. It is replaced by anxiety, awkwardness and rigidity as the sacrosanct bond between personality and greater Self is ruptured. In such a state, in which a human being is out of touch with the bedrock of his existence, inspiration is regarded with suspicion, and effort and complications replace the ease and simplicity characteristic of natural man. This scenario is of course repeated in a thousand different forms from different causes which, however, can be seen to be in essence identically based on the fear which is the consequence of the lack of love of Self.

We have chosen to focus on "demand" as one form of lack of love. By this we mean demands made by others of a soul as well as the demands made by the soul of its own true Self. It should be clear that wherever there is a demand - to be a certain way or do certain things that do not arise from the inner person - there is a lack of oneness and harmony.

In this situation being, rather than welling up spontaneously and joyously and in harmony with the All, is forced. And where being is forced, it becomes laden with emotions such as anxiety, aggression, fear or grievance. A soul taking such demands seriously, whether from others or from its own temporary personality, must be seen to be in a state of schism from Self, as must also a soul making such demands.

We would like to stress that even where souls know better, there is great danger from any tendency to demand of Self or others. The very act of demanding can already disturb any but the most solidly-based harmony of temporary and eternal selves. Even if the discomfort is only temporary, it is unpleasant and could open the door to greater discomfort from any past tendencies to fear or frustration.

Where it is habitual the burden on the soul is such that it can clamp down on the free functioning not just of the emotions but of the body itself, resulting in afflictions such as M.E. - which are of course exacerbated if the diet is not that needed for the person's physiological type.

The remedy lies in jettisoning all the rules, all the expectations, all the standards and obligations, except those freely chosen, and concentrating on the high art of pleasing Self, not others. This means allowing Self to manifest from within rather than being forced into straight-jackets evolved by a largely ignorant outside world. The wise saying from Shakespeare's *Hamlet* cannot be repeated too often: "This above all - to thine own self be true, and it must follow, as the night the day, thou can'st not then be false to any man."

5.10 Opportunity in Catastrophe

In the main, we see great hope springing forth in many situations. It may not always be apparent but behind appearances hearts are changing. Many souls are "catching on" as you would say. They are waking up to the fact that there is a choice; they are realising that they can choose what their hearts tell them rather than what the outside world, or the particular dogmas present in their society, or even their own conditioned thoughts and emotions, may dictate.

Viewing the currents of history on the planet, it is easy to see that the Christian era ushered in a huge wave of undermining of self-esteem and self-confidence. This was not confined to Christianity. Other religions incorporated the only real heresy there could be, apart from the denial of the Self. By this we mean the concept of "sin" which is an extension and correlation of the denial of Self.

In actuality, the conditioning brought about by the concept of sin and the related concept of guilt was an inevitable outcome of the denial of Self on this planet.

The immense wave of negativity which was the result is only now beginning to come to a resolution. Much has been coming out into the fresh free air of public awareness and debate, thanks to the efforts of many brave and pioneering souls.

We say here again so that there can be no doubt: there is no such thing as "sin". There is only experience and learning for each and every soul. Through the consequences of experience the soul learns to distinguish what is light from what is dark. How can the light be known except by knowing the dark?

To be more precise, all is opportunity. When opportunities are missed, when choices are made which lead to the dark rather than to the light, there are still valuable opportunities to realise what is Self through the experience of the misery of not-Self. When the misery is great enough, the soul raises its eyes to what it earlier scorned in its pride and self-will, and begins to realise that there is another choice.

Everything is opportunity. And everything is a choice to be made until the point is reached when the soul transcends the material level of cause and effect and starts to rise above the limitations of space and time. Those limitations belong purely to the material level. They are not known by the heart. The heart exists outside space and time, and the promptings of the heart originate on the level of pure objectivity where all is positivity. They cut through all dogma, all the machinations of the intellect, all the codes and regulations of society and religion, all the "givens" of conventional wisdom, all the spurious authority of Earth's spurious science.

All such dogmas and constraints are not the living reality of truth but the dead shackles of materiality.

So, as we see more and more hearts awakening, lighting up to their own eternal truth, we are filled with joy. Each light adds to the growing light now searing through the material dimension on Earth and drawing to itself all that is of the light in preparation for the shift to the new world.

24/1/99

5.11 Positive Thought

Man is exposed to attack from various levels and, whilst ignorant of spiritual reality, will consequently suffer mental, emotional and physical agony. The ordinary mortal reaction to this problem is that of retaliation - which demonstrates the Law of Cause and Effect with stark simplicity. We do not have to tell you that aggression, motivated as it is by fear, leads to indisposition, depression and in the end to despair - which is not to deny that despair itself can be the beginning of spiritual salvation.

However, even the merely verbal expression of aggression reflects on both the speaker and the receiver. For in this way a process of reciprocal retaliatory reaction will inevitably be set up and a state of conflagration ensues between, shall we say, two people - two people who are probably fundamentally kind and loving at heart but who will, as a result, find themselves at a loss to know how to retrieve their steps and come to harmony with one another once again.

Now once again visualise the situation. But this time see the injured party transmuting the thoughts of anger into a force of love and transmitting that love to his apparent enemy. Can you not realise the tremendous impact that such an act of transmutation will have on the culprit?

Of course, such a procedure would be the outcome of attained spiritual wisdom. And in the face of it one would clearly understand the significance of the words "Blessed are the meek."

If you can handle your negative thoughts and emotions in this way, you will never have any need to complain about the contents of your subconscious mind, for these are not a reality unless you yourself are their own creator. Remember, you are dealing here with thought and if your thoughts were absent there would be nothing in your subconscious.

5.12 Spilling the Beans

Loving memories have no contra-indications. They tend to support and encourage the one who has them as well as those who listen to the wholesome tales.

This effect is very different from any dwelling on what we have called "the unloving past". The recurrent switching of the mind and emotions into such undermining or even shocking circumstances simply reinforces their hypnotic effect on the personality, and even the soul, impeding progress and blocking freedom.

An antidote is required to counteract the poisonous influence of recurrent negatively-orientated thought. Find yourself a willing and understanding soul whom you can trust. "Spill your beans" to this person, who must be able to keep your confidences private.

From our level we will do what we can to inspire and guide this therapist to show you the way out of your dilemma so that you can taste the joy of being yourself without fear and misgivings.

Believe us, the whole thing is not as difficult as it appears because truth itself is straightforward and simple.

5.13 Transmutation - A Way of Life

Much as you may aspire to reach the state of oneness with your true Self you are, during your earthly sojourn, exposed to the onslaught of diverse negative conditions which penetrate the Earth's atmosphere and humankind itself. It is this effect of thought pollution which you have to learn to live with and overcome in a peaceful way. We are aware of your feelings when you are under such attacks and it would be to your own benefit to give this theme careful consideration.

You will perhaps have noticed that once the disturbance has penetrated your solar plexus nerve centre, the little negative sparks begin to run riot in your physical body. Then it is too late to prevent the after-effects which are only too well known to sensitives. Let it be said again that polluted thought is capable of disturbing the whole of your physical chemistry and can result in several hours or days of utter discomfort and misery.

It is essential to realise that defence against such attack is beyond the capability of the solar plexus centre. It is not, however, beyond the powers of the mind. And it is the mind which must be allowed to play its allotted role in the transmutation of the attacking forces into harmonious and peaceful thoughts.

Transmutation will be the answer to many of your emotional problems. This does not mean that you will be freed entirely from these disturbed feelings. This is because your emotions and your emotional sensitivity and awareness play a very useful and indeed necessary part during your physical incarnation on Earth. Emotion and imagination are very much akin and serve us, who dwell in another dimension, very well.

Your great thinkers and artists - your painters, composers, poets, novelists, your architects, inventors, philosophers, explorers, mystics and so on - found themselves continuously in highly imaginative and emotional states. But they had the knowledge to transmute these feelings creatively - hence your wonderful art treasures, your great musical and other works and your discoveries in science, religion and other fields.

Without the ability to transmute imaginative and emotional states your great works of art, science, philosophy and religion would never have come into existence.

But it is when you have these states of emotion and imagination and do not know how to transmute them that they pollute your system and become the source of much pain and distress.

You can, indeed, become experts in the mastery of life on Earth and of your own selves if you will but allow your properly controlled emotions to play their part in your imaginative presentation of yourselves as Spirit in the here and now of your Earth incarnation. Do not despise your emotions, therefore. It is wisdom to love them and thus be inspired to handle them creatively. Certainly, nothing in life can be overcome through antagonism, anger or distaste, but rather through loving acceptance and understanding.

First you must know that negative thoughts - such as anger, hatred, bitterness and so forth - are, in fact, material conditions and certainly not products of the Spirit. Now, having taken heed of the necessity to meet such negative vibratory disturbances outside the field of your solar plexus, you can, through the proper use of your mind, transmute them into physical matter - and thus, with great delight, cast them safely aside.

To make this clearer, try to imagine the personal "ego" as existing at an essentially "material" level of vibration or frequency. Then think of transmuting it into actual material substance which is to be carefully removed from yourself. And this, in short, is the essential task in regard to the lower self: so to transmute and precipitate it that it can be safely and completely removed. Thus, having emancipated yourself from selfishness, you will be free to enjoy the bliss of self-forgetfulness.

The same process is to be applied to negative oscillations such as envy, jealousy, anger, and so on. Imagine yourself, when threatened by such a frequency, creatively using your mind to transmute and thus precipitate it, so that it can be safely removed from yourself. Never forget that all such negative feelings are of a material frequency - no negative state can ever be of the Spirit. The Spirit, as such, is in itself always positive.

You can see that the question of transmutation is very real and very serious. Indeed, transmutation will not by any means be restricted to that which we have outlined above. No, for it is destined to be used by your future leaders in the field of government itself. And both in the preparation for and with the arrival at that time of world unification, it will facilitate the establishment of the long-awaited world government and eventuate the brotherhood of man.

5.14 Truth in Joy

Time flies by so fast and every moment is precious. Do not waste these precious moments in vain recriminations or regret; do not let them sink under your sadness or your despair or your futile ragings.

Instead, seek in each moment for the joy which resides at its heart; open the moment to the light within that joy and let that light flood your being with its delighted recognition of itself in you, so that the moment fills you with its light and you fill the moment with yours.

In that lies truth and the escape from the prison of time into the freedom and infinite reach of eternity.

For, if you wish it, the light will show you what you need to heal your hurts. It will show you your strength to endure; it will point out to you the necessary action if action is required; it will show you the peace of acceptance deep within you in which all your cares will simply melt and dissolve in the light of understanding who you are in Reality.

Let the light in the moment heal your hurts with its joy, and let that joy carry you into the recognition of yourself as eternal. Watch how all your cares slip onto a lower level in the light of eternity, and a lower and a lower one yet until finally they slip completely out of view and out of your mind; for in the eternal they have no reality and no place.

Darana 2/6/99

5.15 Lifting Up and Over

In dealing with your emotions it will help you greatly to keep a perspective, to realise you are in the world but not of it, to see yourselves as the actors not the costumes.

Such a view makes life so much easier for you. It can lift you out and above your own emotions, your emotional reactions to what is going on in you and around you. This lifting out is not an escape. It is moving closer to, or into, Reality.

The letting out of negative emotions to clear them out of the system has its limits. Personalities can become all too easily hooked into it and eventually find out that this deliberate letting out does not really get them anywhere. It can help at the beginning, but it has a very restricted usefulness.

The procedure of lifting up and over emotional states is of great value. It increases and keeps on increasing the sense of objectivity, not artificially but in actual fact. This kind of knowledge and its practice will and must take over more and more on planet Earth. It ends in laughter and laughter spells the death knell to negativity.

It holds for the greatest tragedies as well as the greatest comedies, to stay with the world of drama. They are all plays on the stage and the truth resides behind them.

15/3/99

Chapter 6
Negativity

Negativity sits in the soul of each of you in the form of fear, rage and rebellion which have not yet found their resolution.

Do not be alarmed at this statement. It is not a judgement on you, nor a condemnation, but a statement of how things are on your planet. It describes the difficulty of the conditions for those of you who want to progress. For not only is the psychic atmosphere around your world wreathed with negative thought and emotion, but you yourselves are afflicted from within, to a greater or lesser extent, by the traumas of your own past.

This we see from our level in the form of specks of darkness in the light of your being. When such an area is ripe for release, it appears to spread and you feel it overwhelming your own consciousness. However, as it spreads it also becomes less intense and, as you understand and let go of the cause or origin, the effect disappears like dew in the dawn.

The situation is that of a post-traumatic stress disorder which affects the entire population of the planet.

Your doctors know of post-traumatic stress disorder as it results from experiences of extreme terror, usually war or violence or disaster. It is much to be welcomed that they have at last recognised the effects of trauma on human functioning and state of being.

However, they have still much to realise about the prevalence of post-traumatic stress disorder. They have much to learn about the extent of trauma in human experience, especially in the pre-natal and post-natal child. A small child or baby has no capacity for words and concepts. It only feels. And when conditions are not right what it feels is terror, a terror and trauma as deep if not deeper than that of the battle-field or disaster site.

For the rest of its life, until it finds resolution, it suffers to a greater or lesser extent from post-traumatic stress disorder.

The fear, anger and rebellion and other negative emotional states this entails sit in the soul and powerfully affect any and all aspects of the sufferer's life. These powerful emotions do not only arise in infancy. They may already have their place in the soul from other incarnations. They may arise from events later in life which in one way or another shock the soul concerned.

However they arise, they sit in the soul, and from this secret place they can direct your energies and your actions. When the darkness is very deep and hidden, your consciousness may not be aware of it. You will do what you do with little conscious awareness. Some may justify their words or deeds in the name of what is right or feels right, of the good of self or others, of the greater good, of country, of God. It may involve self-sabotage, interfering in the karma of others, sacrificing self for others, sacrificing others for self ; it may be maintaining a stagnation; it may involve being passive, or over-active; it may consist of hurting and defrauding and abusing both their fellow man and themselves.

We do not speak here of the unspeakable acts of murder, torture and oppression undertaken by individuals and regimes in the name of state or religion or straightforward greed. None who read these words have anything to do with such primitivity.

But through attempting to provide a rationale for what you may be doing to yourself or others, or by denying it or being unaware of it, or any of the other defences you may employ, you reveal clearly a certain distrust of your own Self. If you truly trust in Self you know that all is as it should be. You know that reality is not what it seems. You know that the Law of Cause and Effect brings everything to resolution with love and utter accuracy.

For in the wonderful Oneness of all things, the negativity within you, within all, is not real. In truth, it is a stepping stone to the realisation of your true reality which is the great truth of peace, love and joy in which all Creation is bathed and in which all delight. It is, if you like, your learning, your pathway to greater realisation, your particular challenge to meet. It gives you the opportunity, by resolving it, to open yourself up increasingly to the wonder and joy of the true Self and the unity and harmony of the Universe in which you live.

But while the inner trauma is still so hidden the conscious self is very far indeed from being able to recognise and accept it, although it is dimly aware that it is there. Thus, it employs various defences, for what lies behind the outer behaviour is felt, deep down, to be terrifying truths.

7/3/99

6.1 Going Positive

As long as the darkness within remains unrecognised it will do its best to bend you to its will. In this it will succeed until you have met the consequences of its effects upon you enough to begin questioning your basic assumptions, assumptions that you barely realised you were making.

This often comes about when in one way or another you hit rock bottom. That point may be in terms of inner despair as much as outer constraints and blockages. At it, the full force of what you are about hits you and shocks you to a standstill, or it arouses you to action, or it overwhelms you until you start to accept and face your enemy within by letting the light in upon the secret places where the darkness hides. It is only when you have suffered enough, that you become ready to face your situation and change it.

This is your opportunity. This is when you have the chance to change course if you have been on a negative course and go positive, or to make a further step along the path of positivity if you have already accepted your own positivity.

Going positive will involve different things for different people. For some of you it may be facing up to the fear behind dependency on a partner, a parent, a friend, a child; it may be facing up to the fear that held you in a work situation that was wrong for you; it may be coming to grips with a tendency to be always doing together with an inability to relax, or with a fear of doing anything that might draw attention to yourself; it may be coming to terms with the longing for a parent which causes you to obsessively seek that ideal other; it may involve getting to grips with lack of confidence or self-esteem or insecurity; it may be to do with letting go of conditions and attitudes that are not right for you; or it may simply sit within you in the form of a vague feeling that there are areas of potential and creativity and direction which are hidden from you.

Whatever may be the specific, the underlying fear and anger and rebellion against Self are up for review. Going positive is simply accepting the ascendancy of the Self and identifying with its eternity rather than with the temporary personality.

The more your positivity increases in terms of self-esteem, self-confidence and trust in your true Self, the less hold darkness can have in your being, and at each increase in positivity it is forced yet further from its lairs.

As darkness emerges from its secret places it is like a black cloud which permeates your consciousness. It colours mood and thought and outlook, and will still attempt to influence your actions unless you hold on to your new knowledge of your reality and refuse to accept any kinship with what has been in you so long and is still a powerful force.

This holds true at any stage of this process. You cannot ignore the darkness. You cannot suppress it. In so doing you will only allow it power over you. It needs to be acknowledged and accepted in the clear light of Self. Under that light of pure objective recognition, it cannot long hold its own for it is revealed as unreal and, worse, uninteresting, and it is then free to disperse.

The process can be extremely painful. It involves the release of long suppressed and very intense emotions. The emergence of the darkness is accompanied by the emergence of these emotions and the pain continues until you are able to let them go. Spiritual psychotherapy helps by identifying the origin of the particular emotion. But it also helps to realise that while you may have these emotions, what you are is not despair, or fear, or rage or whatever it may be, that your true nature is light and joy, peace and love.

Accepting this,at the same time as understanding the origins of the emotions, is the only way out of the mess. As you accept your true nature, you can quite simply parcel up all the emotional mess in your mind and hand it over to your friends on the level of Spirit who will dispose of it for you. By holding on to the truth of who you really are, you open yourself to direct help from your own consciousness or help indirectly from the environment, in whatever way your inner reality sees fit to guide you, as it will once you allow it to.

What we are describing is the process of healing and progress. To try to suppress the emerging darkness and stuff the genie back in the bottle merely perpetuates it. It perpetuates the darkness, what is more, at a time when negativity is ripe for its own transformation, through recognition of its unreality, into the light of new understanding and insight.

7/3/99

6.2 Light, the Superior Force

To identify with darkness, as in believing yourself to be despairing, lonely, suffering, hurt, and so on, gives it a power over you to which it has no right.

Darkness has nothing to do with the Self which is light. In light, there is no place for despair or hurt or vengeance or fear. These, and all the other kin of negativity, have no reality of themselves. Their only reality is that which is given to them by a human soul when it mistakenly invests its identity in them.

Without that they cannot exist. All darkness, all negativity is fuelled by the human soul, and were every soul to turn to its true identity as Spirit, negativity would collapse like a punctured balloon and be no more.

For just as negativity has no existence in its own right, in and of itself, so light is everything there is, the one and only Reality, and everything is of the light.

You may question this and point to the things that humans do to each other and to other species and to Mother Earth herself, and ask if these things can have anything at all to do with light. And of course, they do not - except as a means by which light may know itself better.

Let us explain this. Those who identify deliberately with darkness may believe they are in control and that their way is the right way - it works for them and so they think others must be fools for not following it too. They would be astonished and perhaps mortified to learn that they are instead controlled and used to further, not their own limited, self-centred aims, but the great cause of the light.

This can only be understood in terms of level of consciousness. Those who give themselves to darkness and those who are in the grip of darkness when it lies unknown within them do so on the material level. At a higher level they are eternal Spirits. At that level Spirit is supreme and all the works of darkness on the level of the material have no choice but to serve the ends of the superior force.

Thus, in war, in crime, in oppression, those who need particular experiences for their learning and growth which are not afforded by peace and harmony and plenty are able to find them. At the same time, great tracts of fear and anger and revenge find an opportunity for release. The greater the war or the disaster or the horror, the greater the opportunity. And for many souls, the experience of participating in the vilest aspects of man's inhumanity to man is finally enough to so sicken them that they turn to more positive experiences.

There are souls caught up with self-destruction to such an extent that they incarnate again and again in areas of starvation, of oppression, of torture and similar conditions. Such situations give them the experience they need till, finally, the penny drops and they realise they simply do not need these experiences after all.

Then they will find themselves on a very different journey. For by learning what such experiences were designed, by their own true Selves, to teach them, they render those experiences unnecessary. They are then free to seek very different and much more positive situations which will enable them to start making truly positive contributions to the world in which they live.

In this way, where there are blockages and stagnations, whether on an individual or a group level, clear fresh air is enabled to circulate and there is the opportunity of real change towards the light.

All this is in line with the eternal Law of Cause and Effect. This is a law of love. It operates with unfailing accuracy so that no effect occurs without its due cause, and all causes, by meeting their effects or consequences, help to bring about their own resolution as in the example above.

Negativity, having no motive force or reality of its own, cannot build. It can only destroy. Its works have therefore a very limited lifetime unless supported by massive identifications on the part of a people as in the Communist USSR, or by groups of people such as those who perpetuate the doctrine of "sin" and "guilt", whatever religion or race or colour they may be.

Even in such cases, the system cannot endure. Thus Communism in the USSR had a limited life span, and tolerance in the world increases. It is a part of the triumph of the light that a human soul can endure only so much misery and suffering. At that point, it lets go of its by now unendurable stubbornness. Then its greater reality is finally free to take steps to change what is no longer bearable, and progress once more becomes possible.

Even in the circumstances of the greatest fear, once that point is reached a soul will court death itself to bring about the necessary change. Consider the instances of stagnation round the globe and throughout history, and it is easy to see how fear lies coiled around the heart of the darkness and how the human soul finally awakens to its bondage and acts to free itself. From this also you can see that it is the captive soul or the captive people which must free itself. It cannot be done by another when the captive is not ready for freedom. In such a case it may indeed attain freedom only to bring about a new stagnation as long as its will is not focused clearly and unmistakably upon progress.

The process by which a revolution to change what is abhorred in one system brings about another system with all the worst features of the first is an enduring feature of the history of this planet. It usually comes about through the actions of opportunists who see an advantage for themselves. Yet even in such cases, the process still brings about the release of negativity, and with each new act towards freedom, the range of possibilities increases. Over time darkness becomes ever more besieged and its dominions eroded.

This is the case at the present time as we approach the end of Earth's history of darkness. The process will continue in some form or another even after the change to the new world until all souls are free and reality prevails.

7/3/99

6.3 Negativity and Society

From the above we hope you can see that there is no such thing as pure evil. Not even the most terrible human beings who have ever existed were pure evil. All have in themselves the seeds of the light. And those seeds in all of them will, at some point on the journey of the soul, sprout and grow and draw the soul back on its appointed path to its true glory as part of the great All.

Thus, judging and condemning a person can only be done as part of a practical approach in the case in which an individual is not safe for society and needs to be dealt with appropriately. This would entail the understanding that he is erring from his true nature, and that the individual can only begin to reach a better understanding of himself as he continually meets the consequences of his actions. If he is safe for those around him, then he needs to be free to pursue his course till realisation occurs.

Condemnation and judgement as such achieve little in either case. They arise solely in the absence of real understanding and love in the society as a whole.

As a society grows in light, it becomes increasingly effective in dealing with darkness. No society on Earth is yet capable of dealing with real skill in these matters, for there is not yet any society or land which identifies enough with the truth of the Spirit of man. However, there are some which are more enlightened than others and those societies shine their light in the darkness of the others, thus giving them the opportunity to raise themselves towards greater tolerance and openness. In this we think especially of England, which has long been a light to the world and whose light has shone brightly and still shines even in its present condition.

At this stage in your history it is important for you to understand clearly and unmistakably these questions of light and dark - or "good" and "evil" in your terms, although these are not accurate labels.

Understanding frees you from a very ancient error which has grown into a global negativity and now has reached a turning point. We hope that the facts outlined in these communications will assist you in this.
C.A.Jung.

7/3/99

6.4 Stagnation

Man unfortunately is largely a creature of habits. According to the type of society to which he belongs he will, for example, tend to get up, eat, work, have his pleasures, feel and think as well as meditate and pray according to a given pattern of social conditioning.

Anyone who honestly and carefully observes himself will soon realise what a victim of habits he is - habits which have been induced in him by the general and customary expectations of his family, his social group, his nationality and so forth. The tragedy, however, lies in the results: for the enforced routine of the daily round, the strait-jacket of set emotional expectations and the constricting patterns of thought gradually imprison the soul itself.

To one strictly habituated to the fettering of social conformity, any attempt to get him to step out of his routine of imprisonment will cause discomfort in the soul; for the soul is closely interfused with the body in which it has incarnated, and sensing disturbance, will strongly reject the proposed changes. The danger of such a hypersensitive response lies precisely here, since the rigidity which is the cause of this state of affairs inevitably gives rise to stagnation, the precursor of disease at all levels.

Just as the physical body benefits from exercise, so the body of the emotions, of the mind and of the soul, derive untold benefit from being flexed against the constricting habit patterns of personal and social conditioning.

Physical man needs to be aware of the necessity of becoming and remaining flexible at all levels of awareness and function. Just observe, for instance, how many of you are incarcerated by stereotyped habits of speaking and writing. Yet it is precisely the verbal cliché which shackles man linguistically to deprive his language of the creative freedom which gives it the force of life.

When man has escaped from and risen above the habitual fetters of tradition, custom and personal likes and dislikes, he will find all aspects of his life enriched by the development of progressive variation. As for the caged mortal, however, freedom stalks him like a spectre and challenges the security of his prison from every side. A vast network of fixed habits has entrapped and strangled him. His personality in this state is useless to the Spirit which cannot focus itself through an instrument which has become a mere automaton.

We leave it to you to perceptively apply these thoughts to conflicts within the individual, between individuals and within and between groups such as families, tribes, races, classes, cultures, nations and countries; within and between sciences and schools of learning, philosophy and religion; and between North and South, East and West.

He who is rendered anxious and fearful by the trumpet calls to freedom is dominated by his subconscious mind. Into its convolutions the memories of the past slide easily enough, but they have difficulty flowing out from them again into consciousness.

Here in the subconscious, amidst past memories trapped in stagnation, does habit do its work, untrammelled by the conscious light of day. Thus, habituated to a dead past which drains away his courage, mortal man, in terror of freedom, inevitably stumbles into the tragic fatalities of conflict and disaster.
C.A.Jung.

6.5 Antidotes for Negative States

Imagine that in a row before you are the thought forms of various negative states. Imagine also that opposite each is the antidote for that state. Now let us say that fifth from the left is "jealousy" and "envy" and that this is what has infected you. Clearly, what you will first have to do is to find the antidote opposite it. Then simply absorb that pill of thought through the head centre - not the solar plexus.

This spiritual medicine creates in oneself a positive healing attitude which, like a homeopathic pill, will enable one's own "anti-bodies" to do their work effectively. What you must

understand is that a constant pool or fund of healing thought is always readily available to you. All you have to do is to take the appropriate healing thought into yourself when under the attack of negative forces.
It is useless to react against, or fight, your shortcomings. This activity of the physical brain-mind serves only to render negative penetration more effective. In any event the truth of the matter is that negative thought such as jealousy and envy is a condition of the soul, and the brain-mind is quite unable to reach it.

To get to know the various spiritual antidotes for your states of emotional perturbation would be a study in itself. But as a beginning you may be interested to visualise and write down the various thought powers which you can perceive. Do this with a friend and compare your findings. It would also be a good idea to number these powers. Then when you are next in a negative emotional state, take your refuge in the appropriate healing thought which the name and number should indicate. For example, the antidote for jealousy is joy - number five!

Yes, in developing self-healing in this way you will rid yourselves of all negative emotional thought and become most pleasing to yourselves.

6.6 The Way Out from Under

The hypnotic nature of negativity is quite obvious to the careful observer and to the awakening sufferer. Endless repetition of the same old reaction pattern in response to a cue eventually becomes tiresome and boring. The cue can be a word, a look or a happening which triggers an instant re-experiencing of an old, outlived life situation. This is, of course, the very nature of post-traumatic stress disorder.

The way out of the hypnotic trance state is a greater and greater identification with the true Self, the eternal one, rather than the vulnerable, inner child. The Self acts rather than reacting. It is master of the emotions, not their slave. It is proud and decisive, letting itself be guided by inspiration rather than conformity.

The Self has a great sense of humour and leads and teaches through example. It does not suffer fools gladly and will be outspoken and straightforward when a situation calls for honesty. The risks taken in accordance with inspiration will be found to net the most remarkable results. A tricky situation or personality can be seen to be turned around in an instant. Inspiration knows the right time and conditions for the best results.

The true Self takes many a calculated risk. At times the results may have to be awaited, but can be no less remarkable in the end.

Trust in the Self and with it self-esteem and love of Self can come very rapidly or require much repeated experience. The determination to identify solidly with the true Self helps the process substantially.

6.7 Treatment of Obsessional Thoughts

To be constantly assailed by obsessional thoughts is, regrettably, a very commonplace experience in your "civilisation". Nonetheless, the experience can be very painful and damaging for the thinker. And the longer he indulges in this practice, the more difficult it becomes for him to extricate himself.

Make no mistake about it, these thoughts only come by invitation; they never have a reality of their own. It is useless, therefore, to tell such a sufferer to banish negative thinking, for this method will never result in deliverance.

Here we have to consider the love state of the person concerned. And the remedy lies in helping him to create, within himself, a state of love and joy by encouraging him to concentrate on universal love and its infinite capacity to stimulate within him the development of joy - and the consequent rejection of its opposite which is misery.

"How then", you may ask, "should we proceed to inject love into a tortured soul?" And we would reply that it is done through

constant affirmation of the actuality, but not merely mechanical repetition of the word "love" - together with the acceptance of its reality, the reality of love, by the helper or counsellor, who is then enabled to communicate its effect to the one in need.
This process cannot be achieved in one counselling session. Indeed, it may take quite some time for it to take root. Nonetheless, it will and must be crowned with success in the end, because positivity, when brought into practice, is master of all negativity.

At the same time, the sufferer should be encouraged to give - on a positive level - repeated descriptions of his interpretation of joy. If these procedures are properly carried out, we will guarantee you success in due course. And the results will not be of fleeting duration but will become permanently accepted and embedded in the soul.

You will realise that this truly modern method is not widely recognised on your level. We, however, have tested its effect on souls who have come into our dimension, still accompanied by their long- accustomed negativity, and we have achieved total cure by the method outlined above.

It is a method which is not only completely accepted by our own teachers, but one whose efficacy we have, again and again, tested and proved for ourselves.

Chapter 7

Oh, For the Life of a Sensitive

Oh, for the life of a sensitive! And especially of a sensitive on planet Earth!

Like chalk and cheese, the present state of your planet and the refined sensibilities of the sensitive are of very different natures. One does not fit easily with the other. The world in its current debased state of rank materialism finds it hard to understand the sensitive's very different point of view. It is a point of view which colours every facet of his life, from activities and tastes to general outlook to the frequency level on which he operates. The sensitive, surrounded by the lower order frequencies of the majority of the population of the planet, feels himself to be a stranger in a strange land.

It is with the sensitive we are concerned in these writings, which are unlikely to appeal to the mass of earth humanity. They will however resonate with those who are operating on more elevated frequencies, who are also likely to be older or old souls.

For those of you unfamiliar with such terms we offer a brief word of explanation. The more life experience a soul accumulates over numerous incarnations and the more it benefits from its experiences in terms of insight, understanding and wisdom, the older the soul.

We would say that the great majority of older souls are also sensitives. This is especially true where the soul has been able to use its experiences to progress out of the attachment to the material, which is characteristic of the greater proportion of younger souls, and put its talents and abilities in the service of the spiritual progress of not just himself but also his fellows. Such a soul operates at a higher, more spiritual frequency. It is less immersed and enchained by the material and more capable of responding to a different drum.

The sensitivity to which we refer is not an emotional sensitivity. There are many whose emotions are easily aroused. They weep at the sufferings of humans or animals. But their tears come mostly from an emotional identification with the one who is suffering than from true compassion - which does not tend to this kind of behaviour. The emotional and generally infantile nature of such empathy can be seen in the anger which frequently accompanies the tears.

True compassion is, on the other hand, objective. It does not identify with suffering on the material level but views the situation from the point of view of the Spirit which is aware of the illusory nature of all manifestation. Compassion acts positively and appropriately, whether by sending thoughts of love and strength where they may be needed or whether by dealing with the situation to hand as may best assist the struggling soul or souls concerned.

Those who are emotionally sensitive take things personally and feel acutely any slight or criticism. This kind of sensitivity arises out of unresolved emotional traumas in the individual's past experience. It is also encouraged by the hangover of religions such as Christianity which focus on suffering and self-sacrifice. These again have no link with real compassion for they are betrayals of the strong, proud, joyful and loving Spirit which is the true reality of every individual.

A true sensitive is one who is aware of other levels of consciousness. You sense the thoughts and feelings, not just of other human beings and frequently animals and plants but also of those who have left their bodies, or who are not in the body, and who have their existence in the greater Reality which so many on your planet would prefer to ignore or deny.

But this extra awareness comes at a price. It means that you are more open not just to higher levels of consciousness but also to a great deal which is occurring on lower levels. By this we mean that you are open to the vast pool of negative thought which surrounds your planet, and which originates in the consciousness of its inhabitants.

Against the greater part of this, you will find your defence in your own positivity, in normal conditions. Thus the more positive you are, the more you protect yourself against the barrage of negativity. Positivity, like a shield - but made, like no earthly shield, out of pure light - will ward off the swirls and eddies of free-floating negative thought and emotion. The more you embrace positivity, the stronger your shield. The less there is in you of the negative, the less your vulnerability to its attempts to hook into you and bring you down to its own level.

Positivity must be understood as a state of being. You cannot bring about a greater positivity by intellectual exercises. It comes only and solely from identification with the proud, loving and joyful eternal Self, and, as part of that identification, given the conditions on your planet, from the practice of eternal vigilance; for negativity will attempt to undermine you and cast you down from your throne at every turn. As your identification with joy and the eternal in you increases, negativity will have less and less success, retreating baffled and frustrated as a sword glances off the smooth rounded surface of a good shield.

For make no mistake, negativity is your enemy. It works, tirelessly, ceaselessly, to seek out every chink by which it may gain entry and hook into and destroy whatever you are about which is of the positive. Any Achilles heel must therefore be dealt with. Any leak in the barrier of light around you which protects you gives negativity the chance it seeks and it will take it immediately.

You will know when this happens, because you will find yourself feeling drained, depressed and low, and lacking in energy. Only when the leak is repaired can you find again your vitality and merriment.

How do such leaks arise? Simply as a consequence of any lapse in your vigilance and your positivity and your outward focus. Whenever you hold on to a negative thought, a negative state, or a negative impression from the past, you open up chinks in your armour. Not only can negativity then gain an entrance, but your wonderful protective positivity cannot bridge the gap and maintain your state of being on a positive level until a determined effort is made to identify and remove the source of the leak.

This constant probing and attack produces its effects throughout all of planet Earth. Many souls are easy prey and give negativity the chance it seeks to spread its lies and destruction. In doing so, it blocks and blights the potential in the soul as well as the efforts of positivity to build and construct and create, and bring about peace, harmony and joy.

30/1/99

7.1 Spiritual Hygiene

It is the lot of the sensitive to be especially aware of negativity, particularly any build-up in the population brought about by events and conditions. For this reason, you must pay great attention to the conditions in which you live, the company you keep, even the kind of entertainment you choose. You cannot thrive in the company of negative people. Should you share your home with those who are prey to negativity you will find all your efforts are required to maintain your positivity in those conditions, so that it becomes almost impossible for you to make real progress.

We need to consider the effects of mental and emotional pollution. Your mind and your emotions are central to healthy physical functioning and to the healthy unfolding of your potential and aims for your incarnation. But they can also be subject to pollution just as with the body.

If you could see your world from our point of view you would understand this very graphically. Surrounding your lovely planet and almost obscuring its beauty are unpleasant darkish clouds, rather like the kind of smog that used to be seen around industrial areas of cities in your developed countries. These are not material clouds. They exist on the psychic level and comprise the thoughts and emotions of earth humanity. Were your consciousness to approach them, you would feel nauseated. Should they penetrate your defences of positivity and joy they would overwhelm you with depression, with fear, with rage, with weakness, in short, with all the ills which beset this humanity and which stem from the darkness it has embraced for so long.

Each of you in your daily lives is at risk from the negativity wreathing your planet. The emotions and thoughts you have are not always yours. All too often someone else's fear or rage or jealousy or other dark emotion will beat against your citadel and attempt to traduce you to its darkness. All too frequently, thoughts which are not yours will penetrate your consciousness and lead you to behave in ways which are not part of your positive orientation. They may even be thoughts and attitudes imbibed from your mother and father right at the beginning of your life.

Life on Earth is a maze you run, with negativity from your own traumas compounded by the ages-old negativity of your world and the negativity of others constantly trying to lead you from the bright thread that shows you the way forward.

It is an immutable truth that wherever positivity is active on your planet, negativity is at hand to attack it and its works. That means that whenever you are going forward on a positive path, especially when you are beginning to embrace positivity after having struggled all your life with your post-traumatic stress disorder, you are the target of negativity in all its guises.

It is instructive to consider the guises of negativity. They are many, and they range from the obviously negative to what has been described by J R Tolkien in his *Lord of the Rings* as what “seems fair but feels foul”.Negativity is adept at using the mixture of truth and falsehood to trip the unwary. It is its most successful ploy which it has used to undermine the truth of all of the world’s religions, as well as the integrity of scientific endeavour. The lie of

negativity is packaged in apparently unanswerable truths so that it is swallowed like you swallow a pill.
As your positivity increases, its light will show up the darkness wherever it tries to approach you. Otherwise, you may know negativity from the fact that it cannot create - it can only destroy. It creates nothing new where it has destroyed, unlike positivity which is all about creation and the constructive. Where positivity cannot at first construct or create, it may sweep away what exists but only to make room for something new. Negativity can only sweep away; it offers nothing new or creative to take the place of the old.

The only defence against negativity is continuously checking with your own internal truth and the peace, joy and love which characterise it. The more you know and turn to your own truth, the more obvious becomes the lie of negativity like vipers hissing at the heart of apparent wholesomeness. The price of freedom is eternal vigilance - at least until the planet shifts on to a different level and negativity is left behind to seek its own truth.

But psychic self-defence has a number of practical aspects which will help in the time before your new dawn. There is much you can do to improve your environment and your relationships so that the impact of negativity on your efforts is diminished or removed.

Maintaining your centredness in your own being, as we have discussed earlier, is paramount to what we may call spiritual hygiene. Paramount too is your willingness to take the opportunities that come your way to continually progress, whether these are about facing up to old fears and letting go of the past, or whether they involve taking new challenges and embracing freedom - the freedom to be and do that which your Spirit wishes, without constraint.

Living this way allows your positivity to guide and guard you at all times. But it is also of great importance to ensure that those who surround you are also positive and on your own level and making progress. All too often, fine channels and healers are rendered unable to work with us and fulfil themselves because they are in marriages or partnerships or friendships or family or work situations that keep them in an undermined or stagnant state of being.

The importance of "keeping your nest clean" cannot be stressed enough. See your home as a temple which is the outer reflection of your glorious Spirit and therefore sacrosanct. Just as you would not sully a lovely home with dirt and mud, so you should also avoid polluting a beautiful temple with the unclean energies and muddy stagnation of those who are not on your path.

Nor can you thrive and fly as you must if you subject yourself to books and television and films and music that excite your emotions at the expense of your peace and your inspiration as so much of your present-day culture does - and indeed intends to do.

Your sensitivity is a precious talent which you have earned through long and hard effort and experience. The more you see it as such and protect and nurture and value it, the more it will serve you well and help you to make the progress your soul longs for.

26/5/99

7.2 Dementia

Dementia is the response of the brain when it is unable to fulfil its true function which is to act as a receiving and relaying station for what comes to it from higher levels of the individual's being.

Wherever such impulses are blocked, and for whatever reason, the brain is directly affected for it depends for its functioning and health on the flow from the level of Reality. This flow has the effect of renewing and regenerating the physical structures of the brain and is vital for its well-being and efficiency.

Many factors can impede the flow. However, they mostly result from the stultifying and blocking effects of fear and its wide and varied brood of emotions, including rage and rebellion.

Fear itself, leading to suppression and repression of emotions, is one of the rime causes of impairment of brain functioning.

More than almost any other organ, except perhaps the heart, the brain is sensitive to the level of incoming energy, and is therefore all too easily affected when the frequency is too gross for its delicate structures and their attunement. Thus all emotional frequencies when they are not rapidly given off are injurious, as is also an excess of intellectual functioning. The effects are greatly amplified when there is little attunement to higher frequencies and thus little in the way of influx of higher energies and the restorative influences of those levels.

This situation is a recipe for disaster, and the brain will eventually fail in its proper functioning and develop one of a number of conditions which are classed under dementia or, in the most severe cases, an actual physical deficiency of parts of the brain or a tumour.

All energy utilisation in the incarnation ultimately impacts on the brain and heart. So where the energies are of the highest, the conditions aid and support the physical being which is then bathed in the correct life-giving and life-enhancing frequencies of the spiritual level, or level of Reality.

Lesser energies ultimately harm the sensitive receiving and transmitting station which is what the entire physical body truly is and as which it finds its true fulfilment.

25/6/98

Chapter 8

The Law of Cause and Effect

For proper consideration of this subject, it is necessary to be aware that each of you has had many other lifetimes on planet Earth and, most likely, on other planets as well.

You were not then the person or personality you are now. You had different parents, were men or women at different times, were brought up in other cultures, customs, languages, belief systems. However, your soul, the permanent Self, the spark of divinity which is the life force itself, was there. It exposed itself to many circumstances, trying to learn to get control of the given personality so that it could deal constructively with every experience, every opportunity and fulfil the aims of the incarnation.

Often the soul's success at controlling the personality was patchy or incomplete. At times it was not possible at all. This planetary humanity has been at odds with positivity for a very long time. Just as day follows night, the seasons each other and the flood tide the ebb, so has man his own rhythms, as indeed has all Creation.

Some understanding of the nature of rhythm should be acquired by all students of truth. With this will dawn the realisation that the logic of rhythm, as apprehended through the clarity of abstract truth, is in its fundamentals quite unalterable. In short, rhythm is harmony and law, and the effects of each and every fulfilment or violation of that basic order will be impartially operative in terms of the nature of that which has been set in motion.

If the rhythmic harmonic of law were to be clearly portrayed, then before your understanding would be revealed the nature of that perfect measure which in classical times was so aptly termed the golden mean. To consciously observe the precise working out of the law of rhythm would not be possible for your intellect in your present state of physical incarnation. Nevertheless, in the more enlightened spheres of life there is an acknowledgement and understanding of this law which, of course, is also vital to the functioning of your planet Earth, your present lack of comprehension and acknowledgement of its workings notwithstanding.

All abstract conceptions, which are perceived as such on the mortal level, have their concrete counterparts on a higher frequency of consciousness. However, you in your physical body will have to be content to intuit this truth spiritually rather than to perceive it mentally.

Whether understood or not, transgression of the law of rhythm results in the release of unforeseen powers of abnormality which, once they have thus been allowed entrance, cannot be returned to their source. Indeed, nothing can then stop the consequent process of destruction, which is the way in which such abnormal powers are themselves eventually disintegrated into their own ultimate or essential particles or essences and thus finally rendered harmless. Let it be clearly understood that once you have "whistled up the wind" to quote an apt phrase from folk-lore, you will have to bear the effects of having thus evoked it, whether these are to your liking or not. These effects will persist until the "wind" in taking its natural course, has blown itself out completely.

Man's responsibility for his violation of natural and spiritual law cannot ever be abrogated. Nor can the results of his thoughts and actions simply be cancelled as if they had never been. So he must reap the consequences of his negligence in respect to the laws of rhythm. Thus is it inescapable that the "last jot and tittle" be paid for. And those of you with understanding will see in this a great blessing for which you will be truly grateful to the Great Spirit.

Periodic releases of abnormality, created by mass transgression of the natural law, occur on a large scale. The effects of this have become apparent in your world in massive and telling ways. Man in his higher consciousness, however, is aware of the Law of Cause and Effect and is very careful to keep this awareness always to the fore. But where the personality is not under the ascendancy of the Spirit and obedient to its sensing, the physical human being becomes a prey to negativity and thereby contributes to the aforementioned tragedy of mass transgression.

It is a spiritual command that man should elevate himself to a point of oneness where all his thoughts and actions would be in line with the rhythm and harmony of the Cosmos. We who convey this are aware of the ultimate divinity of man, the unity of all being and the supreme dominion of the law of rhythm, as upheld by that Source from which all issues and to which all will ultimately return.

8.1 Law and Health

No amount of physical culture and medication can ever eradicate frustrations and complexes if the mind is working overtime pitying itself for past experiences. We would urge and implore all those who seek to be of spiritual service to begin a trend of positive thought and assiduously to cultivate it. Let us then find within you only those thoughts worthy of your desire to be of service - thoughts worthy of cultivation.

As the Spirit achieves full dominion over your physical self, all sensations of discomfort in the body must and will disappear, for the Spirit is positive thought. We can, on the contrary, assure you too that contemplation of any part of the body, when executed in a negative way, can disorder the contemplated part and create a sensation of pain and disorder. Experiment with your big toe. Tell yourself and it that it is sick and painful, and surely this condition will begin to register before long. (Do not forget to reassure yourself and your big toe that all is well with it after you have conducted this experiment.)

The same is also the case with the internal parts of the body.

Indeed, you can literally will yourself to feel discomfort, and if you persist you can cause yourself an acute illness. Thus, you need to contemplate your own Spirit - not your body - in all its perfection, so that spiritual perfection may be made manifest in your physical being.

Law which is the Creator and the Creator Who is law is the cause of effect. Yet you may well wonder whether you have to be creative as far as your own sowing is concerned, or whether law operates eternally and requires only your passive cooperation. We say to you that if you sow a seed with the motive of self gain for a future time or date you have sown amiss. This truth, dear reader, should be quite clear to you by now. There is no need for you to prepare your own destiny by your good deeds; rather should you accept the effect of the cause in which you find yourself. And through your acceptance of this effect you, in all humility, sow the correct seed for your next harvest.

"Well", you may remark, "does this not mean that I can sit down and do nothing?" But no, my friend, this is not so, as law requires your participation in its execution. And your strength, in preparation for the next effect of a cause, lies in your complete acceptance of it and your whole-hearted participation in it at a given time.

8.2 The Law of Cause and Effect as Love in Action

The atrocity of the elimination of whole populations and the driving out of peoples from their homeland which you are seeing so often repeated at this time has, in fact, happened countless times on planet Earth.

Most of the instances are not known in the history of modern man. What also tends to be forgotten is that, as you view these things, you identify with the persecuted and forget that the Law of Cause and Effect does not err, that there is no such thing as a coincidence.

Those who are today being persecuted are not being punished. They are being given the opportunity to overcome something which they brought with them from a time in which they were busy on the other side of the fence, driving out some other population. Now they have to feel what it is like to be in that situation themselves in order to unload the thought matter which they still carry with them.

However terrible this experience looks from the material point of view, it is nothing but opportunity. It is an opportunity for the soul to come clean, as it were, to learn to become re-identified with its true Self. All the destruction which takes place is only on the level of appearances, not on the level of the soul itself.

This is not easy for many of you to understand. It is understandable that so many of you tend to identify with the underdog, but this identification does not follow the truth of what lies behind the events. These things still have to work themselves out, and they will do so. You on Earth are surrounded by opportunities to stop identifying with such events, to stop identifying with matter and to realise you are eternal, not as personalities, but as Spirit and, as such, part of All there is.

Not all of you have the same understanding. So many are afraid. But instead of being afraid of negativity, you are afraid of the truth because of the kind of conditioning to which you have been subjected. You are afraid to come free.

Yet as soon as you understand the infinite love behind the Law of Cause and Effect which allows you to free yourselves from all that brings you down, holds you back and makes you miserable by meeting it face to face, so to speak, you will be amazed that you spent so long in fear instead of joy.

2/4/99

8.3 Two Case Histories

Love without Prejudice

Martina was in a marriage she was not enjoying. She wanted to be able to "do her own thing", but was too passive to make the changes necessary. She was quickly and easily tired, and often felt depressed.

To change her life situation she needed to first change her diet. It was too high in carbohydrates. She had a history of repeated iron deficiency anaemia. To get enough "oomph" to tackle her challenges she had to start eating a diet that would suit her particular physiological requirements.

Martina's mother had wanted a boy, not a girl, as she had two girls already. Little Martina felt utterly rejected and ill-received. She grew up feeling inadequate and undesirable.

Her mother's rejection of her because she was a girl was based on a former incarnation. In this life, Martina was a man who looked upon the females in his household as an inferior species, blaming his wife for the birth of several daughters. The former wife was now her mother in her present life. Martina was giving herself the opportunity to learn to love herself without prejudice.

She saw the funny side of the sequence of the events. With that, the ice was broken and she was able to go forward towards fulfilling herself.

Panic Attacks

Ralph had lost his job and become self-employed as a painter and decorator. He was suffering from a sense of confusion about himself and increasing panic attacks of unknown cause.

He was born the fourth of five children. His father had rheumatic heart disease which was slowly worsening so that he became more and more incapable of being a real father to his children. When Ralph was nine, his father died of heart failure.

The mother had not been able to form a loving bond with her younger children as she faced widowhood with increasing certainty. She raised them, making sure that they were aware of her great self-sacrifice on their behalf. Ralph had little self-esteem, although it increased through his becoming self-employed.

His panic attacks occurred whenever "I get held up so that I can't get home on time", a frequent occurrence in his line of work. The origin was identified as a great shock when he was eight years old. Ralph remembered that at that age his clothes had caught fire from an electric heater nearby, and that his elder brother had quickly wrapped him in a carpet to put the flames out. But he had been badly burned and was hospitalised for some time. No-one had time to go and see him. He felt exiled as well as suffering terrible pain.

He was now suffering from what was formerly called shell shock and is today termed post-traumatic stress disorder. Whenever he was unable to get home on time this cued him subconsciously into that horrendous experience as a boy.

Ralph had never realised the connection which had him subconsciously hypnotised into constant re-plays of the feelings connected with the original experience. Once he saw what was happening, he could henceforward live his life without this nasty burden.

Ralph had for years been profoundly interested in some methods of complementary medicine, and had acquired training in them. With a background in other lifetimes as a healer of various descriptions, he was getting ready to fulfil himself in this way once again. Having understood and recovered from his own shell shock, he was in an excellent position to help others get rid of theirs.

8.4 Present Thoughts of a Former Revolutionary

No thought is without its origin; no thought fails to find its consequence. All thought works out its destiny through the interplay of thought which takes place through incarnation.

My friends, do not take the business of incarnation so seriously. That is to believe that the play is the reality and to forget that the actors have their own purposes in taking part in the play and their own life outside it. Each actor plays many parts. Sometimes he is a hero, sometimes a villain; sometimes he is the unrecognised motive force behind the events; sometimes he is buffeted by the story. It does not matter. Each part has its place within the whole and each has its own purpose.

As good actors it is our duty and our joy to let that role unfold as it must and speak the lines as they are given. Yet how many of us question our part, and hesitate over it. But consider: it is not in Lady Macbeth's character to start asking herself "Should I really be doing this?" and re-writing her role in the middle of the play. The drama cannot then unfold as it must, and Lady Macbeth will have to start from the beginning and repeat the role until she gets it right.

Please do not misunderstand me, friends. I am not saying that Lady Macbeth *must* involve herself in murder. The plays of Spirit in incarnation are far more complex and far more flexible than any written by any incarnated being, even Shakespeare. Lady Macbeth could well have a flash of insight and realise that what she is about in the play has nothing to do with who she truly is. That realisation changes the whole play instantly. In that insight she has risen above herself and the play now takes place on another level entirely.

But where a true change of heart is lacking, it avails her nought if she has second thoughts. The darkness within must either be released or transcended.

What I am trying to say is that there is only one rule for a good actor on the world stage and that is to be himself, to be, as Shakespeare puts it, true to Self, whatever the state of selfhood may be.

This world has been plagued by the wholesale placing of restrictions on selfhood for countless ages.

I do not speak of restrictions in force in societies with the aim of protecting good citizens against murderers, rapists and thieves.

I speak of the restrictions upon being, enforced by, mostly, the major religions of the world, and by particular moralities of particular societies at particular periods of history. I speak of all the spoken and unspoken strictures by which members of a society can be measured and found wanting.

In your times, in your western world, you speak of political correctness and morality. These are all influenced by the legacy of Christianity which defines certain behaviours and attitudes as virtues, and certain others as worthy only of condemnation and rejection.

Reflect on this, my friends. This is not about crimes. This kind of condemnation and rejection is applied to the failure to be what society considers to be acceptable. Thus, you have the petty "sins" of social class, which in my day involved ostracising and sneering at those who were not nobles or the wealthy.

Today you have come around full circle so that, in your land, a person who does *not* speak with a common accent and conduct himself in an unrefined manner is not taken seriously and is despised. Nothing could illustrate this better than your present-day view that opera, which was composed for the masses, is now the almost inaccessible province of the elite.

As I say these are petty examples. They are, however, indicative of more extreme and destructive pressures to conformity. What are these? They include the perceived worthiness of self-sacrifice; the praising of "selflessness"; the exhortations to "love others";

the unspoken approval of expressions of guilt; the disapproval of instances of pride, even success; the elevation of the victimised and the suffering to the level of sainthood; and, most damaging of all, the fundamental assumption that what you are all about is being a "good" - or acceptable - person rather than a "bad" - or unacceptable - person.

Every single one of these involves an injunction to be and behave in a certain way - which is not necessarily the way you would be or would choose to be if free to do so. The self-sacrificer suppresses his intuition and self-determination and becomes more and more resentful and distressed. The "selfless" one tries so hard not to be selfish that Self is ignored altogether. Loving others if you do not love yourself is impossible. Feeling guilty means distrusting yourself so that all you are and do is subject to doubt. Condemning natural pride and success undermines your joy in Self and the freedom of Self to fulfil its potential. And trying to be acceptable according to the definition of the day involves rejecting or suppressing all you consider to be unacceptable in you, but which may well be more truly you and therefore better than the "good" you are attempting to embrace.

Any and all such exhortations and standards act to block the flow of Selfhood, that is to say, the spontaneous expression and initiative and creativity of the true Self. It is as though in place of the pure, clear light of the true Self you were to set up an altogether inferior mass-produced image and try to express that image rather than allowing the light within you to shine unimpeded.

The consequences can be disastrous.

My own case illustrates this well. I am by nature a philosopher. I have fought for liberty and truth with words and ideas and the sword in many lives. Yet the evil words of "sin" and "guilt" ensnared me in a life many ages ago when I had done what I had to and fought the enemy who would destroy all that I had built and all I believed in - and had to watch those dearest to me die in the attempt, as I did myself.

In one of the lives which followed I found myself as a member of a sect which cultivated truth but whose understanding was based on guilt with consequent hypocrisy - the Cathars in France. In that life I, with my fellows, was most cruelly persecuted and burned. I met my death with abject fear and with deep feelings of guilt and anger.

Still later, I took on a life as a young man from a poor family who was given to the Catholic Church as a novice monk. It was a silent order and the noviciate and daily life were harsh and unbending. There was no ease, no spontaneity, no laughter. I and my fellows were brainwashed with guilt and sin. I was made to know myself as all wrong and worth not a scrap to the uncaring, unfeeling, inhuman machinery of the system. I had to suppress all in me that was proud, strong, vital and fun-loving. I was conditioned to fear, to hard work and to suffering and persecution, all in the name of virtue. The whole of that life was given to the suppression of all that was free and expressive in me. Even though I sought some compensation in rising to the top of the system, it was a life of utter lack of real achievement and joy.

No wonder then that, as Robespierre at the time of the Revolution in France, I was completely unable to freely and joyfully be myself. I carried within me the constrictions and the drive to impossible perfection of the monastery. I carried also, deep down, fear and rage and resentment so strong that, although deeply suppressed, they emerged despite myself - in the terror and oppression I was involved in unleashing on the land I loved.

It was the last thing I intended. I had a vision of a sun-drenched land where all were free to pursue their destiny as they saw fit; where all were equally entitled to the respect of their fellows according to their merits; where all existed in harmony with God and the world. I felt within me a great love of humanity and a profound sense of the worth of each one. It was not a sense of humanity as it actually was but as I knew it to be on another level, as I had known it on another planet. Humanity as it existed was not something I could connect with easily if at all.

I struggled for the words to express what I felt, and they came out coloured by the lifetimes which had gone before. Coming into that life, into circumstances which were not of the best, with such a burden from those other lives, it was torture to me to be myself simply because I could not be who I truly was. All the long-held guilt, anger and fear were making it more and more difficult for me to keep a hold on myself until, while I was still not very old, the words of the madman Rousseau gave me a life-line. Through his philosophy of the natural goodness of man and the transcendence of freedom, I was able to hold on to enough of my true Self and hold at bay enough of the guilt feelings to keep going.

If it had not been for that I believe I could not have sustained the incarnation for very long. The words of Rousseau became my inspiration, and the Revolution brought the cause into which I could channel all of my frustrated expression and leadership and purpose.

Even so, such was the pressure from those previous experiences that I needed all the anchors I could find - in hard work, discipline and fixed habits of thought and action - to keep me going.

Consider, friends, the loving dispensations of the great Creator.

In the Revolution, I had found my cause and my life's purpose and I seized hold of it with all the dogged determination and indeed desperation at my command. I gravitated to the head of what was supposed to be the great Revolution which would be a light to the entire world and to all of history.

But the dream became the most fearful nightmare. The destination was a shining one, but the horses that raced towards it were driven by paranoia, revenge and fear. All were afraid and I was as terrified as anyone else. There were so few of us at the time with the necessary maturity to rise above our pettiness and our passions.

The great enterprise that should have been pursued with single-minded devotion, in a spirit of utmost unity to bring about the dream that was shared by all, was riven by suspicion and division and, divided against itself, it ended by consuming itself.

So why do I speak of divine dispensation?

Because in the theatre which is life on this planet, the nightmare had to be and I, immersed in negativity as I was, yet was one of the instruments of fate in bringing it about.

I know that in that life I was in the grip of a darkness which had its roots in the guilt and terror and rage which had accreted in me over many long centuries. However, the nightmare came about not solely from my own paranoia and desire for revenge for the hurts of ages. Fear and suspicion and division were widespread throughout the land. They arose from the indoctrination of the Catholic Church which taught the people they were sinful and did not matter, that they were nothing.

The Inquisition made of that indoctrination a mortal fear, and by the 1780's the Church and the nobles, with their privileges and corruption and lack of care for the land or its people, came to be seen as the rotten core of all that was wrong and unjust. So much self-seeking and selfishness on the part of those who had so much bred cynicism and abiding resentment in those who had little and were powerless and vulnerable, and who, as a consequence, died in great numbers. There was a deep negativity which had to burst out of the wound like pus to give the opportunity for healing. And in an act of supreme irony, I who preached virtue, I who spoke of love of humanity, I who was known as the Incorruptible, I was the one to throw back the lid of that Pandora's box of vengeance and hatred and fear and death.

The ironies of that life were many. They barely struck me at the time though I smile about them now. There I was, talking of myself as the incarnation of the will of the people, yet fearing others so much that I could hardly bear them near me; I was the spokesman for liberty yet I ushered in the most illiberal and oppressive conditions ever seen in France; I was the mouthpiece for brotherhood, yet I could not love myself, never mind my fellow; and I who once could not contemplate the killing of another human being, who was known for a tender heart and sensitive disposition, yet ended up presiding over a machine of death chilling in its efficiency and terrifying in its voracity.

Yet all those contradictions were true. They were who I was as Robespierre and only as this being with all his contradictions, his different facets, could I play the part required by the times and by the Law of Cause and Effect as it needed to be played.

Friends, reflect on my example. Do you not see here the play of life in all its consummate artistry, its infinitely loving logic and its superlative comedy?

What was so hideous at the time in human eyes, seen from the point of view of the material becomes, from a higher point of view, simply a necessary release of rising tensions so that the country could progress. Monster as I seemed to many at the time, I was no more than an agent of a change that had to be for a stagnant people to be able to move forward. Many as were those who died, including myself, yet in the great in and out of manifestation as ruled by the Law of Cause and Effect, there was not one who had not already chosen his death on the level of his own reality. Many of those who died had caused others to die, in that or other lives, usually unjustly. Thus, coming to death unjustly themselves, they had a valuable opportunity to gain a greater perspective on their actions.

As death comes to all on the level of manifestation, to all in the play, it is not such a great matter. For all return again having learned, we hope, a little more. And in the meantime, the banner of Liberty had been unfurled in a part of the world that had barely known what it was. That, friends, is what endures in this theatre of life. I feel proud that the blackness within me could be used in such a cause, and I too learned much that has enabled me to progress further towards the beacon of truth that continually calls to my soul.

For what is it that the soul needs more than anything else to fulfil itself in incarnation but Liberty, the freedom to be all that is in it and thereby to become the best and highest in itself.

Maximilien Robespierre

6/3/99

8.5 Monastic Hangovers

Many old souls have managed to burden themselves with one or more incarnations in a monastic order, a convent or monastery.

In such cases, de-programming is a necessity to free the soul concerned from the heavy monastic conditioning which acts to limit, if not eliminate, the freedom of the Spirit itself to express, to create, to act and to be and do what it needs to be and do.

Catholic monasticism has been an integral part of Western civilisation for approximately 1700 years, since the time of the Roman Empire. Countless souls have experienced monastic incarnations and been conditioned by them, more or less severely depending upon the order and the state of being of those in charge.

There were various motivations for entering a monastic order. Some young men and women genuinely thought that they would be "serving the Lord" and entered in this idealistic frame of mind. By the time they felt real misgivings about their chosen way of life, most of them were already too heavily indoctrinated and frightened to take their leave. Other candidates were basically angry at and resentful of their elders or at their prospective lot in ordinary life, and sought the apparent security and isolation offered by a monastic institution.

For some, becoming a member of an enclosed order was the nearest thing to suicide, an opting out of "worldly" life and experience, and therefore also of the responsibilities and pitfalls of family life and work. In other words, monasticism for these individuals was an escape.

Others, especially from rural families with large numbers of children, were encouraged from a young age by their parents and the local priest to become the family's contribution to the Church. In many instances the priest would choose the most promising of the youngsters for this dubious honour. No wonder, then, that these young people often spent many unhappy years in this strange confinement which they had not themselves chosen.

Becoming a nun or a monk meant leaving family and friends and throwing in their lot with an assortment of individuals with whom they had often nothing in common, other than that they were members of the same order and inmates of the same institution.

If an individual was an "old soul", i.e. one who had had many lifetimes already, he or she was likely to feel like a fish out of water, different and lonely.

"Old souls" on Earth are few and far between. There are many pupils for every teacher, many sheep for every shepherd. Whether they like it or not, old souls do not, cannot function on the same level of consciousness or understanding or perception as less experienced souls, however hard they try.

"Old souls" who have recently come out of a monastic incarnation more often than not enter into a family grouping in which they are once again the only old soul, thus feeling different and lonely as children already. They may actually have been born to one of their former monastic acquaintances of an older generation. Some interesting pictures emerge from such an action. Having subjected itself to the rigorous and loveless, undermining training of a novice mistress or novice master, sacrificing its own will and freedom in the process, the newly incarnating soul may choose as parent the one who had been the indoctrinating agent the last time. The parent will then usually, quite unconsciously, repeat the same behaviour pattern as before - very little physical contact, no love, much criticism, strict demands for a flawless deportment, no freedom to express emotions, and generally very little meaningful communication.

Often the former novice master/mistress parent does not treat the other children in the same way. It is astounding to see the extent to which past conditioning and relationships from other lifetimes play into the present, especially when non-bonding, hardness and harshness have undermined the incoming soul from the start.

The repetitive nature of these experiences has a positive purpose: having acquired monastic traits through wilful action in another life, the soul strives to get rid of them as soon as possible. What better way than to bring them to the surface once again in the new personality? They are thus made available for de-programming, for they become so disagreeable to the afflicted personality that the latter lets go of its rebellion and is ready to move heaven and earth to get rid of them. At this point, the way to adequate help is shown.

When those afflicted suddenly understand the image of their monastic background and repetitions there is often hearty laughter. The best and fastest results are seen where the funny side of the whole story is perceived. Laughter is indeed the best medicine.

The novice was trained to whatever the novice trainer demanded, however much the task went against the grain, however pointless or repetitive it may have been. And all this with the cooperation of the candidate! Imagine a proud spirit in this predicament. What a perfect waste of precious Earth time and opportunity!

The candidate had to take certain vows. These vows were not always sworn exactly the same in all the different religious orders, but from a practical point of view it is useful to go through the details of the three commonly known vows of Poverty, Obedience and Chastity.

The Vow of Poverty

This generally had nothing to do with the same word applied to economically disadvantaged people or populations. It refers to the artificial concept that, following the vow, the nun or monk was to have no personal private property whatsoever. Whatever there was, was community property. This meant that even the underwear worn was not one's own; that even though one may have worn the same pair of shoes or sandals all year, they were not to be considered one's own. You all know that every animal "owns" its lair, every bird its nest, and will defend it and its contents against usurpers. It is natural to love one's things, find comfort and even delight in them. Such feelings were to be shunned by the monastics. Nothing was to be his or hers.

However, there was at least one order in which the individual members were allowed to own some books. In the next lifetime these souls find themselves to be compulsive buyers and hoarders of books, tapes, records, etc., anything which would symbolically represent the same. But books as such still tend to predominate. A characteristic utterance: "I can't go past a book-shop without going in and buying something. I never get around to reading all I buy but I hold onto them anyway."

In their former life these people had focused all their natural "have and hold" instinct onto their one and only possession. Realising the derivation of their rather expensive habit they are invariably freed from it and can unburden their households of the hoard.

What evidences strongly in the next lifetime is to a considerable extent also influenced by the particular task or duty performed for many years within the religious community. Thus individuals who were employed in acquiring supplies for the institution, in a subsequent life are able to buy something for themselves only if they purchase something of equal value for those nearest to them, usually family.

Some feel compelled to save and mend old clothes they do not want any more and would not even wear. This "disturbance" seems to derive from having been in charge of the wardrobe for the community.

It was considered virtuous to require as little as possible for one's basic personal needs. This leads to an equally personal stinginess the next time round, the individual feeling very uncomfortable if not noticeably guilty about buying and having the little luxuries of daily life.

There are former nuns and monks who feel so badly about the inevitable accumulation of things in their abode that they periodically clear out all but the basic necessities. When they get down to bare walls and simple furniture they feel much easier with this monastic "simplicity" until, over time, things re-accumulate.

Another part of the vow of poverty concerns remuneration for one's goods or services. Man is by nature a trader. Even some of the higher animals trade goods and services with each other and with man. But for the individual member of a monastic community the labourer was definitely not "worthy of his hire". There was no compensatory payment. If an income was derived from the work of the nuns or monks it went straight into the coffers of the institution or the order. The worker responsible saw neither hide nor hair of it and got little or no praise and recognition for their contribution either, in most places.

This customary deprivation expresses in the next life commonly as an inability to relax about money and money matters. It leads to strange and inappropriate disabilities concerning employment, self-employment and doing business.

A good example is that of a woman who had worked for a large company for thirty years. In all that time she had never asked for a rise in pay. "I wouldn't do that." But others all round her had. Neither had she been able to compete or ask for promotion. Yet when promotion was offered to her, she had accepted without difficulty. In exactly the same way, the worker in the monastic situation remains at the bottom of the heap, not seeking improvement unless it is offered, when he can either accept or refuse.

Others have difficulty in having more money and possessions than they actually need at the time. They often compulsively share or give away what they have. They would rather spend money - having it burns a hole in their pocket.

A particular hangover from the vow of poverty is seen in the difficulty, common to spiritual healers, mediums and others of similar occupation, in charging a self-respecting fee for their services. The talent each has is seen as a "God-given gift" which should not be sullied by money. The inappropriate nature of this attitude becomes plain when the individual realises that he or she has built up this "gift" over life-times of devoted effort and experience in the University of Life, as well as in actual universities or through apprenticeships.

In consequence of such misapprehensions, many healers have suffered deprivation in their own lives. They have felt constrained to put out a "begging bowl" in some form for what they call voluntary donations as is so often done in churches. Meanwhile, they are often envious of those who behave in a professional manner.

The fact is that adherence to the vow of poverty does not convey a sense of self-respect. Neither is it suitable for raising the self-respect of the recipient of the services who is often deeply embarrassed by this "something for nothing" experience and gross undervaluation of the Self.

The ancient Greek word "charity" meant love, in its true sense, not debasement of any sort.

The vow of poverty also often causes people in the next incarnation to seek success and then sabotage it, either in the initial setting up of a project or soon after its start. Many are so frightened of success (breaking the old vow) that they run from the mere prospect of prosperity or advancement or independence.

The Vow of Obedience

Life in a monastic order was based on the rule of the order and the rules of the Church, as mediated by those in authority.

The novice master or mistress was obliged to condition the novice to have no will of his or her own. The trainee decided to subjugate it to the commands and requirements of the trainer unquestioningly. Repetitive tasks were imposed which were often purposely senseless and irrational. When the inner Self revolted against the imposition, it was dutifully put down as its stirrings were disobedient and counter-productive to the monastic rule. The trainee had to learn to be obedient to those placed above him or her in the establishment, disregarding personal wishes and feelings. Every time an old soul entered the noviciate chances were that the novice trainer and others were considerably younger souls, thus turning nature on its head, as the older soul is automatically expected to demonstrate leadership rather than subservience.

The vow of obedience consists of three straight-jackets:

1) The "rule" of the order covering day-to-day life 365 days a year;

2) The superiors in the order;

3) The dogma of the Church itself.

The Spirit does not have a look-in - a sad state of affairs, especially when the souls involved imagine themselves to be functioning in the service of God. What God?

As a result of the vow of obedience, former monastics are often plagued by a tendency to self-analysis, to watch and criticise Self continually, usually accompanied by repetitive, over-active word thinking. The harshness of the environment is seen in the harshness with which such a one will come down on himself or herself for some infraction. Many have difficulty sleeping due to compulsively reviewing the day as they had to do as monks or nuns.

Pernicious self-examination and moralising of the Self, calling it to account for everything it thinks, says or does results in a morbid self-consciousness and the fear of doing something wrong in daily life and decision-making.

As the Self, the source of love, is thus prevented from using its vehicle, the personality, in joy and freedom, the latter feels impoverished and deprived in its self-made prison.

The hotly longed-for freedom is feared because of its possible consequences in the monastic setting. Here is where the customary oath "For better or for worse, till death do us part" would be well applied. That is to say, let the frightened, obstreperous personality trustingly relax into the loving and capable arms of the eternal Self which owns it.

The vow of obedience imprisons the Self by clamping down on any tendency to assert and express, any inclination to think and act independently, and can carry over into a subsequent life. Others, in whom anger at the repeated suppression of Self predominates, rebel against perceived authority or rules or limits.

In neither case can the Self regain its ascendancy until the spell of the vow is broken and the sufferer can appreciate the humour of the situation.

The Vow of Chastity

This did, of course, mean that there was to be no intimacy with the opposite sex. In many individuals this leads to corresponding difficulties in the following incarnation.

These may concern the individual himself or herself, or evidence in a spouse who suffers from impotence (more or less) or frigidity of some degree.

However, this vow has other meanings as well. As with the other vows, it covers a vast territory.

The monastic is not allowed to form close friendships with one or more of the others. There must be no personal touch but also no verbal exchange of a personal nature. This leads to a peculiar isolation in the group, and in a subsequent life-time often the inability to form or sustain close personal relationships or partnerships of a non-sexual nature. Some people feel so threatened by such personal, mutual enjoyment that they will avoid it although they long for it, or break it up when it has begun. What a pity!

Silence of a truly artificial nature is part of the system. This, along with the other prohibitions, precludes free and easy communication with others, thereby creating more essential loneliness and deadly seriousness. Still another part of the vow has to do with self-image and projected image. One was not to admire one's own looks or to adorn and beautify oneself in any way. The same uglifying uniform was worn by all and its discomforts and seasonal inappropriateness to be borne without complaint. Bathing, changes of underwear and the like were strictly regulated. There was no room for "Ifeel like."

As a result of this training, former monastics often have trouble making themselves look attractive, wearing colourful clothing or jewellery or other adornments prized by others. They notice their deficiency but cannot explain it to themselves. The whole self-image is deeply disturbed.

Rules and regulations concerning food, as well as a certain emphasis on fasting also work themselves out negatively in their inappropriate carry-over to another incarnation.

Artificially depriving the body and the personality of what it wants was seen as good for the soul, or as a penance. Monastics who fell into this trap later tend to be hard and harsh and depriving in one or another form on themselves. Liking or loving oneself was considered to be the sin of "vanity".

These vows were taken with utter seriousness - breaking them was not to be even contemplated. People have a history of feeling downright uncomfortable when they have broken or are about to break one or other of the vows.

Confession

Every day the monastics attended morning mass which was always the same. Its text contained the famous *Mea Culpa*. In English this is:

"By my fault, by my own most grievous fault, Lord, I am not worthy."

Is it then a surprise that the thoughts so often repeated and in so many ways throughout each day leave a residue in the soul which carries over to other life-times?

A generalised sense of guilt in former monastics is not at all uncommon. However, there is more.

At least once a week, the monastic went to confession with an outside priest who came to the establishment. This confession was not usually a detailed one but it still had to be made and penance doled out by the priest behind the curtain of the confessional. It is not hard to imagine how bored he would have been and how eager to get finished with what he was doing.

In preparation for the event the monastic was required to take stock privately every night before going to bed to see where or how he or she had sinned in thought, word or deed during the day. "Sinned" meant "gone contrary to the rules, regulations, requirements and prohibitions of the system - in thought, word or deed".

This habitual focus on self leads easily to pernicious self-examination in the next life-time with the accompanying judgementalism and moralising.

The result is the absence of relaxed, joyful being, together with the presence of a pathologic self-consciousness.

What a no-win situation, running around in endless circles like a cracked phonograph record, playing and replaying the same old message! Seen in perspective this situation in its entirety is downright comical. Seeing that side of it is the greatest help toward getting rid of the monastic hang-ups.

Here is a proud, pristine Spirit trying to shake off this encumbrance to its progress like a wet dog shakes off water.

Former monastics need to re-learn that life is to be lived, not to be suffered.

Chapter 9

Love

Love sits supreme at the heart of every incarnated being. Sometimes it sits in glory in its incarnation and shines its light through the thin shell of the illusion it wears. Sometimes it sits unrecognised while the shell falls for its own illusory being.

But however it sits, love reigns supreme. None can escape it; none can defeat it; none can destroy it. In the end all errant souls return to their own divinity and allow that divinity its ascendance as the one true Reality, the domain of joy and all that is joyous, all that is true, all that is harmonious.

Love casts its net wide through incarnation, but always it draws its catch back to itself in delighted and delightful reunion. Against the magnificence of love's splendour and beauty the shadows that cloak your world are only fleeting affairs, signifying little in the great light of truth and soon gone.

Think often of love, dear ones. In love you find yourselves in Oneness with all the Universe; and in love you go forth in light and in strength. Nothing is more powerful, nothing is more enduring than love. Nothing is more light, more gentle, more easy.

Reality is love and love is all there is.

9.1 Falling in Love

Dear friends, have you ever wondered why the marvellous feelings you have when you "fall in love" so seldom lead to an equally wonderful and lasting togetherness?

We are sorry to have to point out to you that there is in actuality no such thing as “falling in love”. How can there be when so very few of you know what love is? And when love just does not work that way?

You may object to these statements. But consider carefully what you understand as love. Powerful emotions are powerful emotions. They are not love. Love is nothing more or less than oneness with Self, oneness with the peace and joy and love of the Eternal. Love, then, in human terms is being Self and enjoying being Self.

How can there be love where there is need? What has love to do with self-sacrifice, guilt, criticism of self and others, violence and other negative emotions? How can there be love where there is anxiety and fear?

Love knows none of these except, given the conditions of your planet, fleetingly. Love is serene, self-accepting, pleased with Self and joyful. Love does not “fall in love”. An individual in a state of oneness with himself will, instead of falling in love, simply and joyfully recognise a close affinity on a spiritual level.

“Falling in love” describes an emotional and therefore temporary condition. Usually this is inspired by infantile needs. Where there has been a deprivation of love in early life, the individual may mature physically but emotional growth cannot properly take place. Inside the mature adult body is a young child or even a baby, still desperately needing the loving parent it never had, frozen in time in its fear, its rage and rebellion, its despair. Which predominates will depend on other factors. But together these emotions make up the package which is opened up like a Pandora's box when two people “fall in love”.

When the adult meets another adult who in some way conjures up the depriving parent, that person conjures up too all the unfulfilled needs of the infant, and with them all the infant’s unrealised hopes and longings. The hopes are the hopes of the little one that if only it can be good enough, or right enough in some way then it will win the love it so desperately needs. The wonderful emotional high experienced in this state is that of the inner child which believes that at last it has found the unconditionally loving parent.

But those needs were current many years before the encounter. The situation is unreal. It is based on the past, not the present. It is only where the two souls have a real affinity and also the courage, commitment to Self and necessary insight to resolve their infantile neuroses, that there can be any hope of a good outcome.

All too often one set of powerful infantile emotions and needs simply meets another. There is the glow of hope of the possible satisfaction of those needs, that this time the parental love will flow, and all the aching emptiness inside will be filled.

But after adolescence, the chance of such a "happy ending" has gone. There is no way that the ache of the deprived child can be eased by the love of any other human being. The individual functions like a bath with the plug pulled out. No amount of water poured into it can fill it. No amount of love from another person can satisfy the inner child which never learned to love itself. The plug is that love of Self.

The burden of such needs and emotions upon another soul can be hard to take. It is made much worse by the fact that, as the hope and needs aroused are not fulfilled, as they cannot be, the rage of the desperate and frustrated infant emerges. It may not always emerge as rage. It can emerge also as sulks, as hitting out, as manipulation which includes even threats of suicide, and generally as behaviour which is often a straight imitation or re-play of that of the important adults in childhood.

Where a parent or important adult was critical, undermining, remote, violent, rejecting and so on, the child will often tend to identify with the aggressor who is all-powerful while the child knows itself to be weak and defenceless. In the absence of a positive role model, the child has no other choice.

In later life, these imitations will emerge in situations in which the inner child feels itself to be under threat and vulnerable. These situations are of course most likely to be those in which it finds itself in a close relationship with another human being. But the imitations will emerge to some extent in any situation of power or authority, such as school, or work.

This is the reality of "falling in love" or "being in love". It is quite obvious that love has nothing to do with it, except in so far as the participants may be seeking "love" from each other - without having the slightest idea of what love is.

But some relationships do not give even such token lip-service to love. They are straight re-plays of power struggles from the past in which one or both of the participants seek only to gain power over the other. Frequently the other is reduced to a mere object in such situations. The other becomes a sex object, a "one-night stand", a "sugar daddy", a "toy boy", a "trophy wife" (or husband), and so on. Behind this most cynical of approaches to other human beings lies the deep rage of the infant scorned and rejected to the point at which it has no hope, or dares not admit hope.

A loving relationship shines with harmony, shared aims and loving cooperation . It is above all mature. Difficulties are dealt with honestly and with humour. Fun and laughter are key.

But the "love of a lifetime" all too often descends into a battle-ground or into silence, sulks and hurts. Or it takes its place on a string of "relationships" - in which no-one is truly relating - as the desperate search for love continues.

We would ask: "How can you find love when you do not know what love is? How can you find something which is not outside you but inside, waiting to be discovered and recognised?"

The ignorance of love on planet Earth is matched only by the lack of love among the planet's peoples. People everywhere in both "developed" and "developing" countries (we use the adjectives advisedly) have by now descended so far into the material that they are focused instead on sex.

"Focused" is in fact not a strong enough word to describe the situation. Earth humanity is as obsessed with sex as it is with power. Species of animals are in the throes of extinction because of their use in the production of aphrodisiacs. Large tracts of women-kind are suppressed and hidden from view because their men fear what they see as their power. In truth, what they fear are their own emotional vulnerabilities which they suppress equally. The power play is obvious. In other parts of the world, vast acres of trees are destroyed to feed the appetite for sex magazines; films and television put out more and more programmes featuring sex and violence in the bid for higher audiences; and fashions portray women increasingly as sex objects.

The obsession with sex is as infantile as "falling in love". The overwhelming needs of the deprived infant for love and closeness find a focus, in many cases, in sex as the body matures.

Where the emotions are fully developed and mature, they come under the ascendancy of the Spirit. The need for sex, like the need for love, is no longer felt and no longer has a great significance. How can it in an individual who is identifying with the love and joy of his true Self ? Such a one has no emotional needs as such. He is fulfilled and complete within himself, except for the fact that no man is an island and there is nothing so sweet and enjoyable as the companionship and shared aims of those who are of one's own kind, on one's own level of insight and understanding.

To put it bluntly, the whole business of "falling in love" and the obsession with sex is nothing more than the infantile search for bonding with mummy and daddy taking place planet-wide.

It is a measure of the extent of the fall upon this planet that the very real trauma of earth humanity's lack of love for its little ones is so widespread. It afflicts royalty and Presidents no less than priests and scientists, intellectuals and business leaders, secretaries and nurses, doctors and train drivers, actors and artists - in short, all whether they are rich or poor, black or white, Muslim or Jew or Christian or Hindu, and so forth.

It lies behind all violence, all abuse of others. No-one who has been truly loved from the beginning of his life and who loves himself is likely to become a terrorist or a rapist or a tyrant or a cheat. Hate and fear, rebellion and rage - none of these are compatible with love. Guilt feelings, self-sacrifice, confusion, lack of confidence, moralism - none of these are to be found where there is a healthy self-esteem and self-acceptance.

We can only feel compassion for those afflicted, while turning away from much of their behaviour. We are whole-hearted in our admiration of those who still have such a strong commitment to the inspiration and creativity of the Spirit that they follow it unswervingly despite their affliction. We think of the great souls such as Beethoven and Churchill, and in these times your President Clinton, who focuses on his inspiration no matter what his own emotional trauma, or what his enemies try to do. Such is the strength of his bond with us that he simply refuses to allow negativity of any kind, whether at home or outside it, to deflect him from his task.

Such examples show the power of the Spirit over the emotional traumas of life on planet Earth. They are not alone. There are many, many wonderful souls who are showing others that it is possible to contribute to the progress of the world despite fear, despair and all the other negative emotions. We regret the current, cynical tendency to concentrate on the feet of clay of your great souls. To do so without an iota of comprehension of their achievement in allowing themselves to be inspired over and above their difficulties reflects no credit on those involved.

Others who do not have the same resources as these committed and shining ones or whose trauma is too great, can still find their way out of their difficulties. This is only possible if they too have a commitment to their own reality - to, in fact, love. Where that commitment exists it will work with life from another level of consciousness to bring about events, experiences, and encounters which will assist these souls to liberate themselves from whatever holds them back from the joy of fulfilling the potential within them and committing themselves to that potential.

Often souls who choose this path are destined to help others to do what they have done themselves, using the great resources built up by their own experiences of learning to love Self.

10/1/99

9.2 Love is Joy

There is an old wise saying which states: "As long as you can still be hurt, you do not yet know God."

If this sounds religious, replace the word "God" with words like "All-Consciousness", "All-There-Is", the "Law of Cause and Effect", "Universal Thought" or "Creative Love" so that it makes more sense for you.

However you wish to describe Universal Consciousness, the saying states the simple, basic truth.

As matter is an illusion, the "stuff that dreams are made of", sustained by the love of its Creator, there is really nothing to fear but fear itself.

Let us then, for the sake of understanding, see the material personality with its physical body, its intellect, its emotions, sense organs and hormones as a fine, modern gas stove. The gas which makes it work is the permanent soul, Spirit, light, or whatever you wish to call it. It is by its very nature positivity and cannot mix with negativity. Strong emotions such as fear, anger and hate are negative. Positivity must withdraw from the scene of activity until peace is restored.

When peace is there, all four burners of the stove are brilliantly lit and give out warmth. When negative emotions predominate they clog the pipe so that so little fuel can get through that only the pilot light burns, and even that may grow dim.

A person "on pilot" only will be perceived as dull, boring, dark, lifeless, even repulsive. The true Self, the soul, is not at home. Its sparkle, its warmth, its joy, its humour, its laughter and intelligence are not there.

Love is joy and joy is love and everything there is, seen and unseen, is made of it.

Your kind has made itself miserable for aeons by contradicting this simple fact, in the face of overwhelming evidence against this fiction. If the situation were not so pitiful it would be laughable.

But soon the truth will have overwhelmed the falsehood and all its consequences. For those of you who know it cannot be too soon, or so it seems.

Be content! Many "conversions" to the universal truth are still taking place all over the planet, and the greater the numbers, the greater the joy will be for all.

Remember: love, being reality always wins in the end over illusion and delusion, as light wins over darkness and knowledge over ignorance.

24/9/97

9.3 Loving Kindness

I have to speak to you of love.

This is a word which you should guard closely in your hearts. It is a reality with which you need to surround yourselves in your everyday living, so that as a cloak of great kindness and gentleness and power it protects you, it nurtures you, it supports you and it helps you to be one with your true Self.

Love of Self is a watchword for all those who are in the body. Dear friends, you must guard carefully that you do nothing which does not please you, that you undertake nothing which does not make you feel good and happy and enthusiastic.

You must surround yourselves with only those with whom you can relax and feel content and at one with your Self and with them.

We are very concerned at the lack of love which is everywhere evident in your world. There is a great task to be undertaken to teach loving kindness and gentleness and the high art of being pleased with Self and with life to so many of those people who have no idea of such concepts.

They are simple concepts but they are great ones. We ask you to keep these words in your minds and to put them into practice in your dealings with yourselves and with those with whom you come in contact.

Darana

2/5/99

9.4 Love as an Abstract Motivating Condition

The trials and tribulations of those who serve us which arise through emotional turbulence cause us much amusement - not in a negative way but rather the opposite; because it is through these very experiences that you grow out of the kindergarten to mature in the school of life.

Life experience has many facets that combine mind, body and soul; but it is through coming into close contact with the pitfalls of emotional involvement that you learn, in no uncertain way, the value of detachment.

It may perhaps be a cliché to say that "love conquers all"; nevertheless, this much abused word "love" does, in truth, express within the limitations of your language a vital abstract conception. But love in its real sense as we experience it is first and foremost an abstract state of complete freedom: it is the driving force within us to reach union with the infinite, which brings about in us the ability to raise our consciousness above the limits even of our understanding.

Because you in your present state need an image to help you grasp reality, you are inclined to personify Spirit, to personify even the Creator. By the same token you are in need of a personification to reach an understanding of love. This is where you make your mistake.

We understand love in its true sense as an abstract motivating condition, and so we are able to let it carry us forward simply through the experience of sublime peace. In this state of being, the adoring humility towards infinite wisdom conditions us to experience union with the Great Spirit.

9.5 Love of the Divinity Within

To successfully encourage within yourself the desire to love the divinity within, you would first of all had to have enjoyed the experience of being unreservedly loved by your mother and father or those in *loco parentis* on Earth. For the experience of loving and being loved by your earthly family in infancy and childhood is a precondition for the predisposition to love the divinity within.

Sadly, the practice of loving is not always clearly and unreservedly demonstrated by those who have care of a child. And the lack of this demonstration causes disturbances in the soul of the little one, which it carries within itself into its adult years and after until the very end of its earthly incarnation. Therefore, it is the mission of the spiritual teacher to, first of all, clarify the position of a person towards demonstration of affection, to help him to understand that his parents' lack of understanding and ability to fully demonstrate love was a result of their own misfortune in not having experienced the touch of a loving hand when they came into earthly incarnation themselves.

The whole of your life, feeling, understanding and joy is strongly conditioned by your experiences at the outset of birth and throughout infancy and childhood, as well as conditions at the time of conception and throughout gestation. And herein lies the cause of much sickness in body, mind and soul. So your first principle in helping another should be to sort out any childhood disturbances. But the precondition for doing this is your having sorted out your own.

It is essential for you to do this clearing-out for yourself. And having done so, you can compost the discarded bundle of negative experiences and it will produce an excellent manure with which to fertilise your life's garden. Then will you be liberated from your childhood fantasies and fears. And thereafter, as a free spirit, you will walk tall and unafraid of other people's opinions, attitudes and criticisms.

Chapter 10

Progress

Progress is made at the expense of the demanding self-centred emotionality, the immature inner child. The true adult is outward turned so that the creative impulse can find substantive expression in the world.

As much as the inner child objects to relinquishing its neediness, when it has finally given way to the Spirit's maturity there is a great sense of relief. The feared deprivation turns out to have been of the past. The present is very satisfying.

The future is even more so because the increasing creative expression is not only a support to self-esteem, but enhances it greatly too. There is that feeling of being the "goose that lays the golden eggs" which comes from true positivity.

In fact, the cosmos rejoices every time it is blessed with such riches, be they large or small.

Much of what goes on in and around human beings remains incomprehensible until the inexorable continuity of life in time and space is taken into account.

No thing comes from nothing. The soul seeks to progress. Therefore it does not limit itself to a given incarnation. It needs to unload the heavy baggage of previously acquired unproductive thinking and behaviour patterns and, in their stead, adopt progressive ones.

To be genuinely productive, these must needs comply with the basic spiritual law of the Universe. It is wise to remember that the Spirit is very practical and straightforward. It will achieve its goal in the end. What a comfort that thought can bring you! After all, the Spirit is Reality, while the material, including the physical body with its personality, is a "dream" sequence to enable the Spirit to achieve its aim.

The magnificent simplicity in the scheme of things puts myopic intellectualism to shame.

25/9/97

10.1 The Best and Highest in Yourself

If you consider the proposition the "best and highest in yourself", then many interesting points arise.

The first and most important is that there is no limit to the best and highest in yourself. There cannot be, as the Self is part of the great whole which is Oneness. It is in the Divine as a drop of water is in the ocean, and the Divine is in it as the ocean is in the drop of water.

The best and highest in yourself is in fact a journey, a journey whose first steps involve reaching out of the morass of emotion in which humanity on Earth today is engulfed. It is reaching out of fear, out of frustration and out of rebellion. It is seeking to rise above hopelessness, despair and loneliness, to leave behind self-pity and hurt, jealousy and vindictiveness, and the aggression which masks the poison of fear. It is embracing that in you which is of the eternal; it is following its star wherever it may lead.

Once those steps are taken, once the soul has turned its back on the lowest in itself and set its sights on something more fulfilling and more worthwhile, a path opens up to it and draws it along a brighter way.

For the best and highest in yourself is all joy, all lightness and ease, all shared adventure and loving communication, all determination and purpose.

In the particular conditions prevailing on the planet it is generally true that to keep on track requires great vigilance.

The emotional atmosphere and the deeper emotional conditioning endemic in Earth humanity mean that fear haunts every step taken, and when those steps are towards the light, negativity will use fear and every other negative emotion at its command to sabotage the burgeoning positivity.

Thus to stay on the path and progress along it means not only being on the alert for the downward pull of the emotions, but also being prepared to take your courage in both hands to be and to remain true to Self. Many are the pulls on the individualism and originality of the Self, in particular the rules and customs of society, the pressures of the culture, of other people, of the family, the longing for security and for love. Fear and its followers, anger and self-will, will use them all to keep the genie in the bottle. The result is then a severe tussle between the Self and the temporary personality.

The Self will use every means at its disposal to get its message across to the personality including unusual events, strange illnesses, unexplainable accidents. As long as the personality resists, nothing will go right. Yet, sometimes, where there is a deep negativity in the soul which must run its course the life, paradoxically, may take an apparently successful path. Such success however is designed to assist in bringing home a necessary truth, and as such has its limits. At those limits the reality of the situation emerges in all its stark clarity as the consequences of the accumulated negative actions demand a resolution.

Where there is a battle between the Higher Self and the personality the outcome is not a foregone conclusion. Many continue to resist despite all the efforts of the Self to bring the personality to accept its aims and its guidance, and many are the fallen angels who do not choose to follow its call. But those of you whose commitment to those aims and the truth of your own being is deep and honest and abiding will make it through. You will embark upon the adventure of getting to know the extent of your own greatness, and you will find that, in so doing, you are opening up further channels for its expression in the world which needs it so much. This involves daring and courage to set aside the drag of conditioned social and cultural limitations on originality, to step outside the conventional, the norm, the accepted, the "moral", and to follow a separate but parallel track vis-á-vis the rest of society. It means allowing your dreams to come to the fore and guide you in the face of the outlook and opinions of others. But it does not mean a rebellion against the opinions of others or the mores of church, society and culture for the mere sake of it, for that would be infantile. Rather, it means allowing the deepest aspect of yourself, the true objectivity and maturity of the Spirit, to set your direction; it means giving it the flexibility and commitment it needs to take you to your goal.

There is only one way to do this, and that is by being open to the still small voice inside. This is not the voice of the emotions nor of wishful thinking, which are more strident and less real. It is, as it were, an inner knowing. It is your direction; it is your Self.

And it unrolls your path through life into greater and greater joy and fulfilment and understanding. As you walk that path, your whole sense of yourself changes, and you begin to understand that what you truly are is light and joy and power - the power and light and joy of the eternal Spirit, shot through with love and the purest objectivity of compassion. And as you identify with it and express the Spirit within you, there are more and yet more opportunities which open up yet greater understanding of the truth of who you are, of your place in the great and wonderful scheme of Creation, and of what you can create and achieve in incarnation to the benefit of All there is.

The highest and best in yourself is not a static goal to be achieved. It is a glorious journey back to the Source in which all is one with all else, with achievement beyond your dreams and delight beyond your understanding on the way.

17/7/98

10.2 Pushing Forward

Lasting impressions of all that you do and all that you experience form a large part of your personality, which is the vehicle used by the Spirit to achieve its aims on Earth.

These impressions may be helpful or they may be a hindrance. Where they are helpful, because they are positive, they build up an energy and a light which can be used by the Spirit to make great inroads into its aims of influencing the material dimension.

Where they are negative they accrete as blocks and barriers to progress. Every time the Spirit attempts to go in its chosen direction it meets the block, it comes up against the barrier, and each time the personality balks at that block, that barrier, it makes it more difficult the next time an effort in that direction is attempted.

This is felt on the level of the Spirit, for it is a failure to achieve the aims which are its reason for taking on the incarnation. When the Spirit feels this failure, the personality cannot be happy and its dissatisfactions will increase each time this occurs.

There is a great need and a great push at this time in all those who are balking at such barriers in themselves to go at them head on and not to stop until they have overcome whatever is holding them back.

We are behind this push. You are behind it, for we all work together on the level of Reality. We all have the same aims and we are all aiming at bringing about the new world.

So we say to you: "Do not let yourselves be stopped where you have been stopped before but go forward, push back at all that which holds you back from what you need to be able to accomplish."

Every effort you make to push past old blocks and barriers will be augmented by ten of ours so that together we may overcome and go forward. This is not a time for holding back.

For the truth is that all of you who read these words have put your feet upon a path or have already been on a path for some time. You do not necessarily know where that path might lead, but you keep putting one foot in front of another, letting the path take you where it wants to go.

16/5/99

10.3 Heartfelt Realisations

Heartfelt realisations originating real changes in an individual's state of being are the key to unlock the door to that individual's future.

Nothing more or less than this is required, for this is the hallmark of progress wherever it is to be found operating on a continuous basis.

It is of no consequence to consider the actual state of being itself: this is not the real point which is simply the willingness to change together with a realisation of the necessity of change.

10.4 Security

Makeshift arrangements for doing work are often the only way forward to get a job done. "Security" is an ephemeral concept. There is, in fact, only one security, that of the Spirit.

When bogus security in the earthly sense is adhered to, the Spirit is prevented from progressing because of the imagined need for security, which is simply the fear lodged in uncertainty. The latter is caused by ignorance of the Law of Cause and Effect, and the lack of trust in the reality of the Spirit.

In order to rout out this ancient fear, a prolonged period of uncertainty is necessary so that the individuals caught up in it learn through experience that they can safely let go of their acquired brainwashing. They can then start enjoying the mobility inherent in change.

Many find that, by letting go, a way of creatively fulfilling themselves opens up to them which they had never thought possible while they adhered to the old concepts.

Once again, apparent calamity turns out to be opportunity in disguise.

26/9/97

10.5 Hope

Hope is not a figment of the imagination.

The feeling is based on the deep knowledge of a greater reality than the superficially apparent one in the human mind.

It is also based on the by now usually unconscious recollection of very different conditions on this planet, when brotherhood in harmony was the universal state of being. Individuals knew themselves as Spirit in incarnation, so that love reigned joyfully and easily amongst all.

There is as well the deep knowledge that this condition will return, bringing about your fairy-tale ending of "they all lived happily ever after".

The superficial consciousness, the mind and the emotions, generally misinterpret what a true feeling such as hope is all about. It is therefore often disillusioned, having given in to illusion.

If you let yourself feel hope to its full extent, you will recognise in it a knowledge of certain victory. It will be yours or is yours already, though you may not be fully aware of this fact, having been conditioned "not to pin your hopes too high".

The victory is an inner one. It is the acceptance of your own true eternal being, part of All there is.

22/9/97

10.6 Laughter the Best Medicine

Love is a great creative force and joy is its partner and co-operator. Now consider the sad fact that your earthly world has become almost devoid of joy as humanity is so very prone to wallow in misery. Depression, fear, sickness and complexes such as anxiety, to name only a few, are to be met everywhere in your Earth world - and little does man think of creating in himself his own state of joy.

Yet the acceptance of a state of joy is the motive force for progression. In the state of joy man becomes utterly void of negative influences. Moreover, it is a fact that joy can disperse negativity. Negativity, however, cannot touch joy once it has established itself firmly in man's consciousness.

We often listen to conversations on your human level, and whatever the time of day may be the negative thoughts swirling round your Earth plane are only too readily accepted. One of the favourite topics of human conversation is concern with health and its many disturbances - and here long discussions are held about the speaker's or another's complaints, pains and apprehensions.

Another favourite topic is your monetary misguidance and discomfort. Little does man adhere to the truth that he is as he thinks and that all things come right to those who know and accept this, and hand over the state of the world and their own diseases to their higher Self.

Until man's thought becomes completely revolutionised and he no longer finds pleasure in morbid themes, there cannot be any improvement of any kind in the state of your world. The optimistic, cheerful, joyful and spiritually aware person creates a vibration of light which, in a smaller or larger circumference, touches those with whom he comes into contact.

It is often said that laughter is the best medicine. This is indeed a true saying. We recommend that you all ponder this truth and begin to correct your tendency towards negative thinking. Know that, as you follow this advice, your whole life situation will alter for the better and you yourself will be raised to a higher level through your own effort to be positive in your thinking.

10.7 Action and Counter-action

In all moments and situations of earth life there is opposition. Counter-thought or counter-action cannot be avoided because of the law of attraction. Thus will positivity attract its counterpart, negativity. And negativity will draw to itself positivity as all nature gravitates towards wholeness.

It is not easy for mortal man to delay the negative counterpart for a sufficiently long time so as to establish the positive thought or action before it can be damaged by its opposite. Yes, there is certainly a technique and an art in living your life in the abundance of fullness. And the prerequisite for this is a vigilant spirit, continuously on guard to assert itself with sufficient vigour whenever necessary. Truly has it been said that the price of freedom is eternal vigilance.

We would suggest that whenever you wish to achieve a certain goal in your spiritual striving that you visualise it clearly - and then race towards it in perfect confidence that, in the consciousness of Reality, it is already perfectly realised. As soon as you hesitate or doubt, the impact weakens and the counterpart is enabled to catch up with your thought - and you are no longer able to reach the perfect goal.

We said that life is an art. Perhaps we should rather have said that life is an art of living. Mortal man, on the purely mortal level, is not trained to use spiritual thought. He lives his life in illusion and vain dreams and hence we find dissatisfaction of the spirit in so many persons on your Earth plane. They cannot and will never reach the state of joy which is the ultimate reward of practised higher thought and principle.

10.8 Physician, Heal Thyself

Laughter and frolic are a sine qua non for effective treatment for any chronic condition. The warmth and joy are resident in the heart of the physician and ready to impart themselves to the inmost being of the patient where they find an echo. This may be weak at first, but will soon become loud and clear if the physician makes neither conscious nor unconscious demands on the patient.

To be so relaxed, the physician has to stop making demands upon himself, realising that they are childhood hang-ups or stances carefully acquired in past incarnations.

An example of such demands upon Self is trying to be "good". Man does not perfect himself by endeavouring to do so. His true progression comes unexpectedly. Indeed, he may not even be aware of his own learning until some time has passed when, quite suddenly, he realises he has altered and acquired a higher state of consciousness.

We are a little anxious that so many who work with us spend valuable time trying to make themselves more acceptable to themselves in terms of their conception of what they *should* be, instead of simply being. And we would strongly warn you against too much self-analysis and introspective thought practice. It would be better for you that you should put your physical body to a test of endurance and climb the hills to enjoy nature in all its magnificence. Remember that what you need to have in order to work with us is an unclouded vision and a still and unfettered mind. Music which has an elevating and purifying effect upon your minds and emotions, will also help you to keep yourselves in peak condition for our work with you.

Never forget that you live in a physical world in a physical body and no amount of thinking can ever free you from illusion; for all that you create in your mind is, to a greater or lesser extent, clouded by your inability, while in a physical body, to use your spiritual senses alone. Thus all your thought cannot help but be tainted with untruth as far as Reality is concerned.

To achieve a higher state of consciousness, man needs to experience weakness. If he did not, he would not be able to compare negative and positive feelings. The stronger the feeling the greater the comparison. This necessary experience would be impossible if he spent his time trying to be good.

The harder you try to be "good" or "perfect", the further away from this blissful state you are. You would do much better to simply relax and give vent to your irritations and frustrations in your own particular way until these no longer appeal to you. Then your true goodness will have been brought about without your having fought for it.

In actuality, the attainment of goodness is through the elimination of negative thought and old habits, a process of elimination which is indeed not your business but the business of the Law of Cause and Effect, the greatest therapist there is.

The concept of "free will" is to be considered. Without inner freedom, humour is caged in a prison made of fear, anger and rebellion.

"Physician, heal thyself."

Simply give way to your own eternal Spirit, your own inspiration, in unconditional surrender, and the roadblocks will dissolve into the nothing from which they are manufactured by yourself.

10.9 Fundamental Realities

Time, in your earthly incarnation, is filled with opportunities - and this is continuous. There are no gaps or empty spaces or blanks in time, where opportunity is not.

You earthly people have unfortunately not yet recognised or reached a state of awareness of the richness, the super-abundance of opportunity for progression which the school of life presents.

Perhaps you will ask: "Why should I be forced to learn?" And the answer is that the sum total of experience on the various levels of consciousness serves to make you a whole person and brings about the ultimately desired end - unity with the divinity within.

How then should you react to the infinite variety of stimuli which touch your consciousness incessantly? In this there is a quite simple rule to be observed. Scrutinise the experience and decide into which category it falls.

Is it an irritant? Is it beneficial to your emotional state? Is it a frightening experience? Is it a happy or perhaps a sad sensation? Once you have made the right classification, you can then set into motion an effect which will have an effective consequence upon the cause.

But let us clarify. Take, for example, the effect of anger: to this your reaction should, accordingly, be that of patience and tolerance; to sadness, that of compassion and reassurance; to irritation, that of evasion and retreat; to love, that of loving response. We would advise you to study these fundamental reactions very carefully and think of as many other examples as you possibly can. The examples we have given are indicative of fundamentalities that are assured and follow the tides of spiritual law. With the correct knowledge of fundamental realities, in terms of operative law, you can make heaven on Earth for yourselves and those in contact with you.

The little things in your life which frustrate or irritate you, are often the ones which are the greatest stumbling blocks in your progress. One small sentence can in its effect trigger off a multitude of disastrous happenings in your life. The accusation of a person that you may have acted wrongly or that you are defective in character may completely upset you.

Gradually, however, you will learn to handle such a situation in the proper way, which means allowing the soul or Spirit to cope with your response in this - acknowledging that nothing is apparently too trivial or too small for its attention. Thus you avoid the futility of attempting to cope with your irritations and other upsets from the level of the personality - rather permitting the personality to serve as a bridge for the soul and Spirit to come to grips with your problems on Earth.

The Spirit is a united force. In its tremendous strength it can take over and command the physical body. In the beginning of man's alteration which inclines him and later enables him to offer the Spirit dominion over himself, he still, nevertheless, has a wilful and rebellious attitude. But through the negation of self, the fluttering of the physical body gradually abates until law is obeyed and the "over-soul" has established its dominion.

Once this has been realised, enjoy your vantage point in your physical vehicle and consciously go about your work from your new level of objectivity. This state having been achieved, you cannot ever go back to your earlier manifestation. There is then only progression, but never retrogression, towards the great goal which is complete unity with infinity.

Break not the peace of God by your excessive thoughts and your strivings to progress more quickly and more thoroughly. Man in his natural surroundings would live by the sun and use the darkness for his recuperation in deep sleep. So-called civilised man wastes hours of God force by taking part in "worldly" activities during the hours which have been set aside for sleep - hours which used in the correct way would confer benefits which are quite unimaginable to the so-called civilised human being.

Do not resist your impulse to confess your own weaknesses and failings. The Great Spirit is all-listening and continually transmutes negative thoughts into positive power. Remember that all which is in you of the intake from without has to be eliminated before you can be a truly whole person.

10.10 In No-man s Land

One of man's greatest curses is self-hypnosis. The motivating force in this is a death wish, a preparation for the next downward step which is that of "opting out" completely. It is often practised by the genius who, on getting to the frontier between illusion and Reality, finds that he has neither the stamina nor the courage to take an upward step into the other dimension.

So, having denied his own divinity, he stays in the no-man's land of consciousness, and hard will he find it to go either back or forward, as neither one side nor the other will have sufficient force to attract him.

Numerous souls in physical bodies wander your Earth in a dream state - seemingly unable to assert themselves, incapable of using either their intellect or their spiritual senses sufficiently to create in themselves continued activity for their own satisfaction and for their release from bondage. And each time you help such a soul to awaken you have indeed performed a work of rescue. Such stagnation between two points, in whatever field it may be, is utterly to be condemned. If it is not remedied, it will cause deterioration of the physical mind and the dissolution of the Spirit which, as its ability to hold the body weakens, will gradually withdraw.

Take a politician, for example, who is unable to assert himself on one side or the other and who is therefore in a state of stagnation. In this condition it is inevitable that he will lose the power of creative thought. And because of this he will lose too his sense of self-esteem, with concomitant disturbance in and deterioration of his bodily functioning.

You will find this no-man's land in all conditions of life on Earth. Think of this particularly in regard to the innumerable wreckages in the field of love and marriage and you will find it a clue to much.

It is only in the face of such crippling stagnation that we, on this side do, on occasion, encourage in a human soul in this condition a sensation of utter failure and despair. We do this through our power of thought - and for the purpose of drawing the soul out of its no-man's land of stagnation onto either the positive side of Reality or the negative state of illusion, which is the state of awareness which rests upon the physical senses.

We can also do the opposite and encourage a state of elation in the affected soul. Where the individual understands how to accept this alteration, of which we normally inform him beforehand, he would escape the need to be shot onto the other level. But there is of course, in some cases, a period of tug-of-war before one side or the other gains the victory. Certainly, such intervention is usually necessary only once, for the drastic remedy teaches the one who can thus be rescued from a state of stagnation all he needs to know.

The state of stagnation we have discussed here is the most serious handicap in man's race to find his oneness with his own divinity. But we could not begin to mention all the many detrimental states in which mortal man, with gay abandon, places himself - without forethought and with utter disregard for the consequences.

10.11 Awareness

The basic essential for the realisation of truth is the growth of wisdom. This being understood, it will be grasped that the idea of the search for truth is quite obsolete. It can be said that the apprehension of truth centres itself in the organs of spiritual sensitivity and perception. Of the validity of this statement you will be aware only after you have undergone that development whose ultimate achievement is the realisation of the reality of the soul. Of course, it is precisely the longing of your soul to achieve Oneness which is both the source of and the motivating force for the desire to reach perfection. If, however, your longings are motivated by your intellect, then you will certainly go astray in your "search" for truth.

It is essential that you on Earth, incarnate as you are in physical bodies, learn to separate the intellectual processes from those of spiritual awareness or of the intuition. Unless you do so, you will find yourselves lost in a maze of distorted thought. There you will not be able to see clearly, neither with your inner or your outer organs of sensory perception.

With the latter, your organs of material sensing, we are but little concerned. For the physical brain, upon which you are dependent for their use, is of value only on the material level of functioning. Nonetheless, once you have surrendered to the reality of the soul on its own plane, then your brain itself can be used by your higher Self as an instrument through which service can be rendered to the human race on Earth.

At your present level, however, learn first to locate the frontier which separates "brain" intellect from real awareness. Then you may take that plunge which will enable you to break through into unknown states of consciousness, which is precisely where your adventure begins.

When we listen as we sometimes do to the conversations of incarnate human beings, a great compassion stirs within us in the face of the ignorance of the nature of life revealed by the speakers. It is an ignorance which is largely the result of perception being veiled by matter. Such a situation, because of limitation, creates great difficulty but is highly progressive in effect because of the challenge it provides the incarnate soul to gain dominion over its personality, even within the realm of the material world itself.

But those of you who are close to us do not have the same difficulties as the rest of mankind; for you are in a position where you are able to make a serious attempt not only to reach a state of awareness where you may obtain glimpses of Reality, but to storm heaven itself to gain knowledge of the unknown truth, knowledge which will stand you in good stead for your future work of service. There is therefore much hard work awaiting you, but also indescribable joy.

However, when you begin to contemplate the taking of the necessary steps to reach the heights of awareness mentioned above, then you also become aware of the hindrances dragging at your feet. We intend to deal with two of these hindrances, the first of which may be described as "vacillating in no-man's-land".

Here we have a most frustrating situation. Preparation has been made to cross the "river" which, symbolically speaking, separates one from the land of the truth. The incarnate soul endeavours to remove all obstacles preventing the taking of the plunge, but the personality always balks at the decisive moment, for it does not wish to be submerged in the unknown from which it fears it may never emerge again.

In this situation, neither the physical consciousness nor the spiritual aspiration seems to be able to gain the upper hand. Spiritually inspired psychotherapy is often effective in such cases, if the individual can be directed to an appropriate practitioner.

The second hindrance is irritation. Irritation, which can adversely affect the soul itself, is almost always based on the lack of humility of the physical mind consciousness, the personality consciousness of the sufferer. This lack of humility forces the individual to make comparisons of an invidious nature between himself and those with whom he does not identify, usually those whom he cannot see as fitting into his style or pattern of life. These are therefore rejected as defective in some way or other, or excluded on the grounds that "they are not our kind of person".

The making of such odious comparisons clearly indicates a desire for superiority which is directly related to the lack of humility. This lack is, in turn, the result of a suppressed sense of spiritual failure; hence the compensatory superiority complex.

10.12 Honesty a Greater Truth than Modesty

There are two kinds of will: will and self-will. The former is positive, the latter negative - it stands in the way of progress. The self-will of the personality is a destructive force which will cut across all spiritually premeditated progress and annihilate the consequent material alignment with Oneness.

From the planetary level right down to that of personal slander, habitual criticism - itself a by-product of self-will - can become a deeply ingrained habit. And the consequence of this habit upon the practitioner is indeed unfortunate for, as a result, the consciousness tends to seek for the negative in all situations. The consequence is that the life of such a one becomes a swamp of negativity. It is an addiction that is difficult to cure as it feeds upon its own produce.

Many are much troubled by the thirst for expression in the physical body. This is frequently caused by man's laziness in using his senses for the acquisition of knowledge. Dissatisfaction must needs demonstrate its presence, not only in the mental and emotional, but also in the physical sphere. Both the ridiculous and sublime have their purpose - one would be lost without the other.

Others are even more troubled by fear. This submission to fear is a regressive movement back to the womb. Such a retreat from the pangs of progress requires skilled and inspired counselling. And it is we who have reached Reality who are the inspirers of those who practise it.

Counselling is indeed a living science. Every part of your being has its own work to perform in this particular field. Useless, in the multi-dimensional work of counselling, is dependence upon the physical brain, for it is merely one-dimensional in that it operates only at the level of the physical.

To those of you who cooperate with us we insist that you state and assert to yourselves, day by day, your qualifications on the level of Reality so that you may become more and more aware of the food we deliver to you for distribution amongst the needy ones.

We are tired of your "humility" and "nobleness". These are all human conceptions, created in the mortal brain and not experienced in Reality. They are wasteful and de-energising. Replace them with joy and enjoy your inflated short-comings. Honesty is a greater truth than modesty.

10.13 A Project

The construction of a building is a skilled job. Whoever takes part in its planning, designing and consequent erection must be intense in his longing for perfect workmanship and also reliable in every way in its execution. First comes the thought, which is an inspiration, then the design, and then the work itself. Each member of the team must be in good health and shape, interested in his mission and zealous to surpass himself and others each time the task is a new one.

My friends, this is a ruling for all who have life experience, as each Spirit in personality form has to undertake his own creation whether of thought or matter; all the mortal rules which were, of course, dictated by the infinite wisdom, apply to you also. Nothing can be successful unless the fundamental rules are observed and whatever the task, it must be filled with joy. All decisions taken need to be creative. That is to say, the end result of the decision should be a building up of positive creative power. See in these rules of life a liberation and a stepping out towards greater experience and do not mourn that which you will have had to leave behind.

Consider your own strength a valuable asset for the means of escaping a stagnant situation and to begin a new term. Incarnate man in his preoccupation with the problematic effects of the execution of his desires and decisions can be disturbingly self-centred. This is his handicap. Whilst others fulfil themselves with inner calm and trust, he walks the long way round and gets exhausted.

If you, poor soul, who do not find it possible to raise yourself to the level of the higher consciousness, could only for one second taste the elation which self-denial and loving abandon can produce! Practice letting your Spirit tell you the way. Do this with great humility and feel the unbounded vitality of your higher Self in its wholeness and oneness.

Whilst all this takes place, your intellect can assist you. If it is encouraged to do so it will tell you about the futility of your fears and depressions and it will bring you into the true realisation that your abandon to negativity is a complete negation of life itself.

Hasten to develop your awareness of your Spirit - not through the mind but through the heart. The key to the secret of happiness and joy has long been lost but thought itself can be a substitute for it. As a safe needs a special combination of letters which perform the magic of opening the door, so you can form your own combination to achieve the penetration into the secret shrine.

This is a fairy story. As all such tales are inspired and have a happy ending, so may it be for you.

10.14 Discomfort in the Soul

The irritability of man's mind is an expression of discomfort in the soul. One therefore has to search the soul to find the origin of its displeasure. And such a search may well reveal the cause of the soul's instability to lie in the "eternal field" - as well as in the karmic conditions and influences which surround man on the Earth plane at all times.

Man has become accustomed to consider his problems solely from his own mortal point of view. Spiritual progression, however, enables him to rise above the narrow circumference of his own personality to view his picture of life from the level of the eternal consciousness. This ultimately is the only way in which you can achieve perfection in all things, even though you may still be forced to have your being in a physical body.

You may think this achievement too hard a task; but you may rest assured, nevertheless, that in making this effort you yourself as a living soul in a living body are ineluctably moving towards the realisation of perfection - and you will experience this perfection not only on the spiritual level but also on the physical plane.

This having been accomplished, and by your own endeavours, your life as a whole will reveal that perfection, and your spiritual and material problems will unite in the absolute in complete peace. Thus you would have come to the end of all striving and of all labelling and classification and be perfectly entitled to bathe yourselves in the sunshine and warmth of the eternal being which is the great Creator of All.

Why then, beloved ones, do you not accept this challenge and henceforth go forward with this thought only in your minds - that you may achieve this state of progression? Indeed, not until such time as you fully acknowledge yourself as Spirit in your physical world, though not of it - but in it according to law nevertheless - not until such time will you ever be able to appreciate the beauty and the joy which true spiritual acknowledgement and living can bring you.

We sometimes border on despair at the turmoil, the anxieties, the worries, frustrations and aggravations which befall mortal man in his daily life - yet we cannot interfere! But we can make suggestions and show you the way to lasting joy and peace. And if you should earnestly desire to follow our inspiration we could promise you success in a very short time.

10.15 A State of Perfection

There is a need to show everyone who walks the pathway of spiritual progression that to become stationary in one's individual evolution is like sitting down by the still waters, greatly bothered by thirst yet having neither the energy nor the desire to go to the edge, drink from the pool and be satisfied.

As long as channels or mediums are used to contact only comparatively unevolved souls for information and messages of a personal nature, the true purposes and beauty of communication which can be achieved only at the highest reaches of awareness will not be made known to the seeker - who must always ask himself a very simple question: "Where do I go from here?"

Man in his mortal incarnation has become completely polluted, through his consciousness having been invaded by illusionary frequencies which have become to him an unclean "reality". Can you imagine what a task it is to deliver mortal man from himself and his errors into a state of being where he can receive the actuality of spiritual resonance and thought, which must needs enable him to live a true and perfect life?

A state of perfection is the sublime experience and culmination of man's conscious ascendance to the summit of himself, his complete union with himself, a goal desired by multitudes though only attained by a few. Yet these are not the chosen ones - rather are they the ones who have chosen.

This acquired state of Oneness results in man no longer being aware of himself through his physical body with its senses, and thus ceasing in his consciousness to identify himself with the imperfection of his material being. This attainment fills mortal man with joy, which is not to be identified with happiness, for joy is the equivalent of happiness in the spiritual sense.

When this unity has been achieved we can talk about rebirth or of having become as a child. From this vantage point of perfect unity man can have his being on Earth and act, in all life situations, from the reality of its spiritual significance as apprehended by his spiritual senses alone.

10.16 Unity with Self through Humility

It is not an uncommon state of mortal man to be actually initiated into spiritual reality yet, despite that, to be unaware of spiritual truth and even to repudiate it on the physical plane of consciousness, because of ignorance of the fact of his own knowledge at the Earth level of awareness. Such people are prey to continuous friction between the higher and lower self. As soon as the higher consciousness reaches out, the lower self immediately sets about pulling the progressive soul away from its eventual goal which is the realisation of spiritual truth while in actual physical incarnation.

Man having been born into the particular environment of planet Earth is conditioned right from the start by his parents, brothers and sisters and others who are present in that community. Thus the seed is planted for the future of the child's emotional system. The greater the contamination of the surrounding thought frequencies, the more quickly the mind of the little one becomes negatively affected.

These early thought processes remain deeply embedded in the subconscious mind and play their part in the formation of the child's character, which expresses itself in and through the nervous system. Thus will the growing mortal being suffer the adulteration of its own originally untouched sensory system and very soon the effects of such poisoning become apparent.

In one way or another an over-estimation of the personal self is induced and this causes a lack of self-confidence which results in an inferiority complex. This complex and humility cannot live side by side. Humility being a spiritual quality becomes prey to the negative state of inferiority, and we see the inevitable development of selfishness, greed, fear, anger and many other negative qualities of a like nature.

You may ask how this state of affairs can be altered and brought back into proper alignment. This is solely a matter between man, his personal integrity and his relationship with the Divine. You cannot teach such a person the truth. Nor can you forbid such a one to speak. And even the demonstration of love and true humility will not reach him as the negative quality of his thinking is firmly established in his subconscious mind.

There is, nonetheless, one way in which you may attempt to help such a soul. First establish contact with his higher Self through thought. Once you are sure that this contact has been made, you can then approach this person on a physical level - always remembering, however, to hold your own divinity in sight. Remember too that all the words you speak must be within the grasp of his understanding, yet based on the fact of your own spirituality.

In this way you gradually develop a relationship of love - first of all in earth terms. This is necessary as it would be understandable to our troubled friend. Once you have satisfied him as to the reality of your love you can then proceed to raise his consciousness step by step to the point of no return. Here, at last, he will be safe and unite himself with you in adoration. Thus will you and he walk in the light together. This may be a prolonged task but your first success will be a rewarding experience for you.

We take it that each one of you has been in situations where you have had to say to yourselves: "I can go so far and no farther. More help I cannot give". And this is exactly where you stop to commence a new beginning; because this is the turning point of progress for you and him.

10.17 The Welcome

You cannot imagine the thrill of joy felt on the level of Reality every time an errant soul incarnated on Earth decides to identify with its own eternity, accepting matter as the illusion it is.

Such an event is, indeed, a great homecoming, worthy of a celebration.

This is the real meaning of your story of "the prodigal son" whose return was such a joy to the father. Now imagine the joy upon an errant humanity of a whole planet having decided to finish with its sad experimenting with negativity.

It fills the Oneness with utter delight. The joy of its coming about resounds throughout the whole of Creation. The great All can be again at peace.

25/9/99

Chapter 11

Spirit

The custodian of the secret of life is your Spirit. It can only release that which has become its consciousness according to your maturity. No demanding or expectation can further the release of your Spirit's knowledge or wisdom. The process of gain and letting go is fundamental. It must, however, be recognised and understood by the physical mind after the Spirit has penetrated matter.

This process is as eternal as man himself, and forever will progress show merits in gain and joy on all levels of consciousness. This should be a comforting thought for mortal man, and it should encourage him to learn his lessons well and go forward day by day without looking back. What, however, is man capable of doing or omitting to do to either further or hinder the evolutionary process?

We regret that the majority of dwellers in a physical body are willing to open neither their minds nor their hearts to the truth that man is an eternal being. The distractions of your civilisation are the outcome of the need to still fear and apprehension and to distort or, better said, to diminish the difference between fact and fiction.

As soon as a child reaches the age of ego awareness it begins its fearful stances. Again and again, the consciousness recollects memory patterns, usually of a negative nature. Guilt feelings set in and fear of the justice of Law takes possession of the personality. Man, not recognising his own personality, allows it to pollute his thought and as two thoughts at the same time have no room for expression, the Spirit has to stand back until the personality has finished its antics.
By that time, the negative thought has embedded itself very comfortably in the consciousness and the personality is loath to

let go of it. In the meantime, the Spirit is sending little particles of energy to the consciousness to help it to release the fear. Here we have the continuous tug of war between right and left, or positive and negative. Were this not so, the personality would lose its vitality very quickly and the Spirit its impetus to bother.

There is, however, a third force which we call the neutral one. It is the centre of the emotional see-saw and is by nature balanced and capable of continuously keeping the balance. It is this very thought force which man can use consciously for the purpose of bringing peace between himself and his higher reality, between body and Spirit.

Life must be experienced on all levels of consciousness. All mental states serve as constructive teachers. Laughter, tears, anger, joy, fear, uncertainty and many more useful conditions occur during a life-time in earthly incarnation. These have to be appreciated and accepted. The greater the willingness to come to terms with experiences of a difficult nature, the quicker the lessons will be learned.

We would advise you to stop thinking of that which is happening to you today or tomorrow, and rather listen and feel the moment of calamity as joy. Exaggerated self-interest and analysis become almost obnoxious and certainly extremely boring. To us they appear as patches of darkness in a beautiful light. You will not disturb anyone but yourself and so delay fulfilment. We wish you irritation from your own thinking, because this would be a stimulus for the pause you will have to make in this kind of behaviour, during which you may cultivate an outward-looking attitude.

11.1 The Midas Touch

Many centuries have passed on your planet since humanity ceased to understand the truth behind the old fable of King Midas and his golden touch.

It was not the metal gold which was meant originally, but the transformative and healing power of creative love. It can be seen in action today, apparent to those who can perceive what lies hidden to souls who cannot, will not stop identifying with the illusion of matter.

As those who decide to identify with their eternal Selves thereby become positive, a golden glow surrounds them and a brightness emanates from them which is easily recognised by their fellows.

This is the real gold, the Reality behind the appearance. It will either light up what it touches, or put it to flight if it insists on seeking darkness.

All you who decided long ago to be of the light keep on touching souls who have not yet made up their minds or may still reverse a negative decision if they allow themselves to become fascinated by your brilliance, like an insect by a light at night.

You need not strain. Just be yourselves, confident, joyous and ready to be nudged into action by us whenever there is something we can accomplish together.

8/1/98

11.2 All is One

All words are one. All worlds are one. The Spirit world and space are one. And space is in you as you are in space. Space is not a location but is matter unformed as far as the human eye is concerned.

Never will man be able to discern space with his physical senses. Yet the enigma of space is not unsolvable, for its true nature reveals itself to those who have the enterprise and courage to develop the ability to use their power of spiritual discernment. To such as these will it be revealed that space is inhabited and akin to the Spirit world.

There is no doubt that the time has come for man to admit to himself the true nature of his own reality and to completely accept the sovereignty of spiritual consciousness.

You are standing in the foyer of a grand revolution in thought. However, just as a new-born babe cannot see its mother, cannot focus the power of its vision upon her until certain physical developments have taken place within it, so, similarly, will mortal man have to advance a little further before he will find himself able to focus his own spiritual vision upon the truth of Reality.

In the security of Reality make haste to reach the necessary pre-conditions for the opening of your spiritual eye, for every delay retards the progress of the physical world to its long-awaited transformation.

Discard your painstakingly collected data and calculations concerning the nature of the heavens and the heavenly bodies, for what can you build on ground which shifts, cracks and crumbles in the face of a reality for which there is no possibility of definition in terms of your earthly measurements?

In truth, your mortal concern with matters of space is an impotent futility. Only in thought, in spiritually-inspired pure thought can the answer be found.

11.3 Living on Two Levels

It is often thought that mortal man, to achieve progressive development, must in consciousness leave his mortal existence and become, already in his earthly consciousness, his true Self which is Spirit.

If this were so then your self-imposed physical presence on planet Earth would be completely without purpose. You, as Spirit, have chosen the trials of a life in a physical body which would enable you to learn to cope with the many emotional states which you need to endure and resolve. Through the suffering of the physical and emotional senses your Spirit will be greatly enriched - and it would be very short-sighted if you were to evade this opportunity of learning through these experiences.

You should realise that there is an immense opportunity for experience on your earth plane. And, indeed, the greater the tension of the senses the greater will be the relaxation that will occur as a result of the discovery and application of the new knowledge towards which life experience drives you.

What do we mean concerning the value of earth experience? For instance, you talk very glibly about the word "love"! But love, in the sense of mortal experience, results in the complete union of man and woman - and holds within itself the lesson of giving and sharing and thus learning the beauty of selflessness on that particular dimension. Love in the spiritual sense is the complete union of personality and Spirit with infinity - and likewise leads to self-forgetting. If you have chosen an earthly existence in a physical body, you are at liberty to choose the experience which leads to the state of Oneness in the physical sense.

It is just as the great teacher Jesus proclaimed, that "in God's house there are many mansions", and your earthly sphere is one of them. Indeed, it certainly serves as a valuable school for the scholar, for this world gives him the opportunity to experience all kinds of emotional situations. These in time will induce great strength and maturity in the seeker.

It is not advisable that man should wish to escape or evade these experiences so as to withdraw completely into the safety of Spirit. Rather should he face up to his problems with courage and joy and see in every turmoil and difficulty another stepping-stone toward eternal peace.

Your worldly life is not to be wasted but is to be loved and enjoyed. Stand up for that which you know to be true and right but, like Jesus, chase out of the temple those who dare to challenge your integrity. Do not be afraid of confrontation. Even Jesus used his emotional body to drive away from his presence those who persisted in the transgression of divine law.

More and more will those who serve us and in divers ways have to learn to live their lives on two levels - and furthermore, to accustom themselves to the fact that they will no longer be unreservedly accepted by those who are merely members of the Earth community; for the Earthling will sense that one who serves spiritually can no longer fit into the Earth community to be completely at one with them there.

But let not yourselves be troubled that those of the mundane world will no longer accept you as being one with them or one of them. Many persons that you have met and will meet walk the same path as you and live also on two dimensions. You have recognised them silently but knowingly. There are many who serve in different and various ways that we may succeed in our joint aims.

Such servers will have to be careful not to let their thinking be completely in one dimension only. It is essential that each one achieve an absolute balance, for each dimension has its own centralised magnetic force, and if you went too near that centre you would be overwhelmingly attracted and drawn away from the centre of your own equilibrium.

If, for example, you were drawn to a spiritual dimension too strongly, you may find it almost impossible to return to your own point of balance and the world would then completely reject you. It is important that you think this over very carefully so that its full meaning, and the practical implications thereof, be fully grasped.

11.4 Two Subconscious Minds

All experiences and thoughts are registered in your subconscious mind. And here we refer to experience and thought on the physical level. But spiritual experiences are also registered in a subconscious mind. However, the latter has its reality on the spiritual level; for thought of a spiritual frequency cannot be registered in the subconscious of that instrument of physical level mentation called the brain.

So you see, you do indeed possess two subconscious minds - one on the physical and another on the spiritual level. To bring the thoughts recorded in the spiritual subconscious out of hiding, so to say, you need a "cooperator". Just as a gramophone record needs the help of a needle to vibrate engraved sound events into the audible sounds of words and music, so is a spiritual "needle" a necessity to bring to life events stored in the spiritual subconscious. But remember that the cooperating stylus is on the spiritual level, no physical thing but a concept which will assist you to bring recorded thought into sensory life.

Here on the spiritual level the indispensable cooperator would be love. And this is so because no other conception is able to release your spiritual recordings. Once again we may have told you something which may be difficult for you to accept. But remember that love is a sublime positive power and the key to all human success on the level of spiritual consciousness.

11.5 "Tuning In"

It always takes courage to propagate new ideas and new ways of thinking. But remember, beloved ones, that truth also progresses and does not stand still. Let your minds be flexible and do not reject that which does not meet with your agreement, because sooner or later, especially when you come over to our side, you will have to alter your concepts in more ways than one.

Take for example the speculation and theories of your philosophers and scientists on the question of time. Profound as you may consider these to be, we who have passed over have, nonetheless, had to make radical alterations to our conceptions in this regard. Indeed, so fundamental has been the change we have had to make in our conception of time that we would be unable to explain it to even advanced thinkers on your Earth, for their mental processes would not be adapted to our present understanding. Nevertheless, you can take the point that we who are here have had to learn to think in a totally new manner.

Now, bearing this in mind, we wish to consider the concept of tuning in. We often hear it said by you, "Tune in to that which is highest in yourself" or "Tune in to God". If these words are spoken to the uninitiated they leave the receiver in a state of disillusion or, better said, muddle, because to one who is on the mortal level of understanding the above words are useless - such a one cannot form any idea of their true meaning in regard to himself.

The secret of "tuning in" successfully lies first and foremost in the state of being in which you may find yourself at that given moment. If your mind is obsessed by earthly problems or polluted by thought waves of a lower nature you cannot reach an attunement with higher frequencies. So first of all, you have to get yourself into a state of "loving" - loving all that surrounds you in your immediate vicinity and also as far as your thoughts can reach out.

The experience of loving has to take place on various levels of consciousness. Herein lies the difficulty for you as mortal beings who are forced to love in a physical body and yet aspire to the purely spiritual environment. It is only when the entire you has found its oneness or wholeness in love that you can take the next step towards attunement (at-one-ment) with your higher Self.

We advise that you honestly meditate upon these thoughts. It is necessary to undergo this meditation before you can really experience what we mean by the thought of loving on all levels in relationship to your at-one-ment (attunement) with the divinity within.

11.6 Inspiration

A correct posture whether sitting or standing is invaluable. However, such a development is best assured through a discipline which clears the head by way of a proper control of the mind; the prerequisite for this is spiritual surrender - the subordination of the personality to the hegemony of the Spirit.

The difficulty in the realisation of such an achievement is great for a materially-orientated person because of the density of thought, which serves to block the mind from being used as a clear channel of communication for the transmission of teaching from the higher levels of spiritual frequency.

The majority of those on your Earth who call themselves human beings appear incapable - and even reject the possibility - of reaching that state of relaxed surrender and spiritually poised equilibrium in which the mind can be used as a channel for higher thought.

And so, too, is it with mediocre sensitives, those professional channels who, notwithstanding their claims, have but sparse and very meagre awareness of spiritual thought. Even this impoverished contact is given but scanty access to the mind because of their primarily emotional polarisation.

Such limited link-up, without any proper mental concentration, defeats the true purpose of communication. The inevitable result is that confused and muddy thought patterns are permitted entrance, to inhabit the mind and, in that unclean state to reign there.

Such a state of mind can never be clear and strong enough to withstand and overcome negativity. In its inefficiency and insufficiency it will tend to fall prey to confusion, the source of all disorder and, in the last analysis, of disaster. Therefore all its attempts at creation will produce nothing but a shambles.

We would urge you to clear your mind of negative thought so that Spirit may be encouraged to fully occupy that space. This is a tremendous undertaking and many are the disciplines which have been used in order to arrive at that state.

What we, however, would propose, though by no means easy, is highly effective in its simplicity. Set aside a period convenient to you when you may be quiet for a while. Then determinedly, yet quite calmly, refuse to entertain any thoughts which may come into your mind from outside, including those arising from memory, emotional fancy or the intellect. Patiently persist in this practice and you will eventually reach the point where nothing from without will be there to distract you from receiving from within.

When you have sufficiently settled your karmic debts and have set about cleaning up your physical body so that it may truly be a temple for your Spirit, then those who are the appointed representatives of your individuality or entity will come to you and speak and make themselves known to you. In doing this they will help prepare you for the treading of the path towards the eventual mastery of yourself by your own Spirit, your own true Self.

Before this can be achieved, however, we will take you gently and lovingly by the hand to lead you upon a journey that you will first have to undergo, and then upon another and still yet another, for there are many such journeys in the life-time of a human being if the goal is to be achieved.

Therefore, you will trustingly place your hand in ours and, to begin with, will leave behind the emotional patterns that have hitherto dominated your life, in the knowledge that the abandonment of yourself to the domination of the emotions creates errors in the incarnated soul itself. About this we wish you to be firm and strong. So do not pity yourself when you are forced to abdicate from attachment to emotional conditions.

Be at peace with yourself and do not prostitute your many sensitivities. For whenever you do this, you must halt your journey until we have helped you to clear up such mistakes. Better is it that you straighten the way of your progress by coming to us as a whole person. Such wholeness is in your unity with the divinity within and not in your devotion to and adoration of a guide, adept or master. Understandably, of course, your conception of that divinity is not ours, as the nature of our perception is different from yours - so different, indeed, that no human language could describe our experiences.

That we involve ourselves in your development results in a quickening of change in you. Many of the changes initiated will have to be undergone in your physical body as well. Indeed you, who read these writings, will have gone some way along this path and have come to the level where a book of this nature strikes a resonant note of meaning within you. Perhaps you are rapidly emerging from a state of negative involvement and are thereby undergoing a positive change of image through the reassertion of yourself as a whole human being in society. Such a development is the outcome of the colossal strength which spiritual thought gives to man in an earthly body.

Having comprehended this you will, henceforth, no longer be so much identified with your experiences and your involvement in them. Rather will you be standing above them. In passing from one level to another, you can in all situations exercise detachment and with clarity observe and be aware of yourself from a higher point of vantage. Thus will you be able to enjoy that freedom which being in your world but not of it will bring you.

This too you shall go beyond. And so, on that second stage of your journey, you will have your first great experience of joy. About this we, of necessity, must remain silent, for your language is quite incapable of communicating such an experience. However, we would appeal to all those who study our words and meditate upon what we say to remember these thoughts. Know also that an apple never falls very far from its point of origin, which is its tree of life. So, should the touch of death enable you to enact the role of a falling fruit, you would not come to rest far from your source. Thus would you soon find your own true kith and kin who, of course, are not of matter. The joy of that reunion is unspeakable.

It is high time that you let go of all compulsive thought and allowed the joy of positivity to prevail. Why not replace your own density of thought with our clarity by coming to us through your surrender to your own Spirit? Remember, we are you, for we represent your own true Self. And in union with us you will know and your knowledge will be as a road sign to you.

So many of you are confusedly running from one school of occult and spiritual thought to another. But whether it be the study of the esoteric effect of diet, herbs and potions, witchcraft, sorcery and magic, astrology, flying saucer phenomena, the various presentations of The Ancient Wisdom Teachings, or other intriguing patterns of occult thought and investigation, these will have little place in the life of those who are seriously studying our writings - not, that is, at the moment, though they may be properly considered later on.

Do not mistake us. Occult studies are not to be shunned, for they are as true as life itself. But too many cooks spoil the broth, and it is the acquisition of simplicity which is the prerequisite for progress. This it is which will prepare you to become clear channels for your own reality and, in the first instance, for those who are to act as intermediaries for you on its behalf.

The tragic fact of the human situation today is that, having abandoned his innocent trust in simplicity which enables Reality to be grasped directly, man has become lost in a maze of his own making. To the consternation of the wiser ones, he now prizes complexity and all because of having lost the ability to think in an uncomplicated manner.

Hypnotised by complexity, his mind has become so cluttered that he is unable to recognise the simple truth and is blind to the enormity of the mess he is in. He is, in short, spell-bound.

Yet once again, the force which would enable him to achieve the breaking of that spell is love - not in the mortal sense of the word, but love as a spiritually stimulating force which would altogether dispel the negative state of complexity, and gently lead modern man into subordinating his egotistical little personality to the control of that which is highest and best in him, his own true Self.

11.7 Living in the Light

Once you have developed the awareness of the reality we call Spirit, you then live your life to a great extent on that blessed level of consciousness. And in that state of awareness, you are in true communication with dwellers in that realm of light. This is an exciting and elevating feeling and in time you accept this state of peace, confidence and health.

Only when you have learned to master both the mortal and the spiritual state of existence can you function completely as a channel for the transmission of healing, truth and advice. Acting as a channel or medium demands a perfect knowledge of your responsibility, not only towards man but, furthermore, towards the Divine.

Mankind must awaken to the truth that the purpose of healing and mediumship is not one of satisfying the personal desires and ego of the sitter, but to help the seeker to progress spiritually in such a way that he in turn becomes capable of raising his own consciousness to the light, to the state of unity with All there is, through which all will eventually become expressions of perfection at all levels.

This will not only bring such a one into a state of joyous living but will also enable him to inculcate in his fellow man the desire to emulate his way of life. Think how quickly such purposeful development would spread in ever increasing circles over your plane of being on Earth.

As long as you accept channelling, or mediumship, as responding primarily to the demands of the mortal consciousness you will never know the "Kingdom of Heaven", and you will not be joyous nor partake of the blessing and pleasure of a perfectly healthy mind and body, but will remain a prey to all frequencies which are negative in nature, character and quality.

11.8 Elevation to a Greater Awareness

Elevation to a level of greater awareness is a joy to the soul of the individual concerned as well as to all of us here.

It is in this way that the material level is enabled to become a more true reflection of the spiritual. The progress of even one soul lifts the material closer to truth.

When this occurs with many souls, the upliftment is so great that a whole world consciousness is advanced beyond its former achievement and takes on a new incarnation.
This is not a frequent event in the great Universe but it is a shining goal for souls on many worlds. The reward of such efforts is much desired, for they bring an extra dimension of progress that the soul would otherwise be unable to achieve.

Such an advancement can only be brought about by many souls working together. It requires that the conditions of the world be those which either necessitate the attempt or will aid it. And it requires effort over a long period of time to bring about. But so glorious is the enterprise and so wonderful the results that many are eager to embark upon the adventure.

This was the case with your planet. The fall of the planetary peoples from oneness with the All was so devastating in its impact upon this lovely world, that it was decided that the conditions were right and the attempt must be made.

The conditions, though not usual in such attempts, were those of a vast investment of negative energy which could be harnessed to the effort and thus power it to success. This is to say that the higher levels could catch the negative energy on the hop, as it were, and deflect it into wider purposes than those for which it was intended.

To put it another way, the negativity was so great that it brought about a backlash which would act to restore the balance. But not just restore it. The backlash was used to fuel the undertaking of raising the planet to a higher level of awareness.

Once the negative force was well-established through giving it full rein in a directed fashion, it could be used as one uses a motion at its fullest extent to power a return in a slingshot effect. As this took hold the working of the Law of Cause and Effect began to speed up. The stagnations that beset the world were being forced to clear. The main stagnations are those in the form of oppressive regimes and dogmas and conditioned thought which prevent the individual from pursuing his own experience and learning and purpose, as was and is the birthright of the individual throughout the inhabited Universe.

Such stagnations include dictatorships, totalitarianism, communism, socialism, science and religion and all such systems which require the closing of the mind and the closing off of opportunity and freedom and choice.

Throughout the history of the planet since the fall into time the individual has been oppressed and controlled. Primitive societies, of recent times, even sacrificed their own people to propitiate gods whose anger would otherwise be unleashed upon them. What terrible gods who need to be appeased by human, or any, sacrifice! What fearsome beings who would attack those in their care!

Here already could be seen the extent and grip of the alienation of Earth humanity from itself, projecting its fear upon the loving Universe. Here those whose inadequacies required that they dominate others saw their chance for power and climbed on the fears of their fellows. Here it is more than apparent that entire peoples had sunk from the eternal to the depths of the material.

Yet the recent history of the planet charts an inexorable rise of the individual through feudal systems and dictatorships and all the other oppressions of majorities by a minority to reclaim his power. The land of England showed the way and has shone a light for other nations for many centuries. The Civil War embodied many themes which were taken up in the American War of Independence and the French Revolution and grew and spread thereafter. Yet such was the extent of negativity that it was a race against time. The load of guilt and fear and rage and hatred stoked up in the recesses of consciousness around the globe had been steadily increasing. There was a point at which the fate of humanity hung by a thread.

Then the great lady in England came to power, and the opening up and clearing out of the Augean stables of Earth humanity could at last proceed. Together with the two other great souls she opened up the deepest stagnation of all and pushed this planet's humanity upon its forward path to a degree for which we hardly dared hope.

As the individual began increasingly to find his voice and his right to his own self-determination, and vast areas of negativity began to clear, a new world has come gradually into being on another level. Its manifestation came about as soul after soul made the leap of realisation and in doing so added to the construction on the level of Reality.

Their inspiration came from souls such as we and you, and all old souls who have given their efforts down the ages to raise the peoples of the Earth back to their true level.

There are matters still to be resolved in the old world. Negativity is losing ground but still has more than one sting in its tail.

But the new world waits, glowing, for the final shift from the old world to take place.

Then indeed will history end and joy begin.

9/2/99

11.9 Destiny

Destiny calls all those whose being has raised or aspires to raise itself to other levels than the purely material.

Such souls have spent many lifetimes acquiring the wisdom and insight that are the result of countless experiences. They may be truly characterised as mature souls, fit to lead and light the way for others who are seeking their own progress out of matter and into Reality.

Their knowledge and deep understanding and insight give such souls the stepping stones necessary for their quest. The light of their true Selves touches the truth in others and draws them towards the abiding joy and fulfilment of the reality within them.

Theirs is a precious task, a wonderful responsibility, the most fulfilling service they can offer to their world.

It is, simply, to be true to themselves and to allow the goal which is in them to unfold and guide their footsteps on the way they must go, so that they light the way for others to follow.

Neither institutionalised religion, nor the philosophies of cynicism and despair, nor any organised, systematised body of beliefs can slake the thirst in searching souls which is for the ever-changing, ever-flexible, ever-abiding eternal truth of being.

What is this truth? Why simply that all are part of the Divine and exist in the Oneness of all Creation; that all are free to follow where their inner truth leads; and that all inner truths combine in the glory of the unfolding of Creation which is the Divine plan.

Spontaneity, initiative, creativity, and the joy and peace and love which lie at the heart of truth - these are the hallmarks of Spirit in incarnation. Truth sweeps aside all rigidities; it sweeps away all the childish stances so beloved of Earth humanity; it washes away infantile rebellion and hate and anger; it drives out fear absolutely.

Only this can slake the thirst, the longing in humanity. And it is the destiny of every wise old soul to act as a light and show the way to those who thirst, to show them the light in themselves which is their way.

Destiny always calls the old soul. Now, however, the call is all the more insistent as time swirls in ever narrowing circles to its rendezvous with eternity.

31/3/99

Chapter 12

The Greater Perspective

The evidence of our contributions to life on Earth will slowly become understood as more and more minds upon the planet wake up into welcome objectivity.

As mind-sets are shed, what before was seen to be impossible now begins to assume dimensions of probability. And probability will bring such a thrill to minds which had closed themselves off from contact with other planetary humanities, except on their own extremely primitive terms. We have never been prepared to communicate on those levels which we deem beneath you, never mind us!

In truth, the history of human populations upon this planet was set in motion by those of us who are accepted to act in such matters. When we saw how things were developing upon the planet, we realised that here on Earth we had a very specialised situation which would be ideally suited for a particular solution for which we had been praying for some time.

To explain this, you need to realise that life in incarnation is always an opportunity - and as such always involves choice. The process of materialisation of the Divine Spirit is a great miracle. It offers an unparalleled opportunity for the creative Spirit to manifest its supremacy in the most direct manner, by raising matter to its own level so that lowly matter reflects the glory of Spirit.

There is a vast discrepancy between the high fast frequencies of Spirit and the very dense and much lower vibrations of material life. To infuse the material and mould it to express the ineffable, the inexplicable, the infinite and eternal - what a task! And what a joy to succeed in that task! What a celebration of the Spirit and what a unique manner in which to explore its many facets!

This is the wonder and the glory of incarnation. So you have poets whose words stir the eternal in the soul. You have musicians whose notes raise the soul beyond its earthly confines. You have artists who bring the heavenly to uplift the mortal consciousness.

But creativity is not restricted to the creative arts. It is a process of being open to inspiration, to the promptings of the Spirit, in all material endeavours. Leaders in the fields of politics, commerce, education, science, finance and medicine can be equally inspired. A butcher may display as much creativity as an artist; a mother may equal a musician for inspiration and the light she brings to her task of raising children. In human interaction and endeavours of all kinds there are unlimited opportunities for inspiration and creativity. A life painted directly by the incarnate Spirit will shine in dazzling beauty no matter what kind of canvas is used.

The opportunity of incarnation is not taken by all. Many become prey to the lure of the material and begin to fall from oneness with their eternity into the little world of time. In most cases, on most worlds, these lapses are lovingly corrected and serve to highlight the lesser nature of the material compared with the spiritual.

But in some instances, the soul becomes enamoured of its own power on the material level. It begins to believe that it has found a new way, or a better way. It has, of course, found nothing of the kind. What it has found is a debased sense of its own importance and power which can then rapidly cause it to become mired on the level of the ego - the temporary personality.

This is the problem that we faced on several inhabited worlds many aeons ago, by your reckoning. Where there is little or no recognition of the extreme danger confronted by the soul in this situation, there comes a point when there is nothing any of us can do to retrieve matters. Our concern is then to find a way to remove such souls from the rest of the humanity, to whom they become an affliction and a liability.

This was not an easy matter to resolve for various reasons. But when we saw the same symptoms in the then humanity on Earth we realised where the solution lay. It was clear that the affliction needed to be worked through on its own, much lower, level, and that to do this those affected had to be removed from the positive environment of those whose orientation remained of the highest. They had to be given the freedom necessary for their affliction to run its course.

We must make it clear to you that to you today those souls would hardly appear affected in the way we describe. So diminished has humanity become in these times that you would be blind to the signs which were all too clear to us. You would see, dare we say, gods where we saw fallen angels. This gives you some idea of how great has been the fall. And certainly, at its beginning, it took many ages for the shining qualities of the eternal and infinite in those souls to ebb away. Yet there was a certain point we learned to recognise at which the future orientation was already set and could no longer be deflected.

At that point we had to act, and with the agreement of the Earth Spirit, such fallen angels were brought to this planet. There were complaints about such a displacement, but in Earth we found the most beautiful planetary being and the most loving planetary heart, and the planet formed from this most loving heart was beautiful with a beauty to touch all hearts. It floated in blue-green serenity and not one who complained did so again once he saw his new home.

We ourselves oversaw the settlement, and we took care of our settlers and guided them for as long as they needed our assistance. This was some time for they were still not fallen completely into time, the last limit for the soul before fully embracing the material. As long as they still recognised themselves, even if only dimly, they accepted our direction.

However, when we saw that their self-will and pride were attaining dangerous heights within them, we had to withdraw for our own safety, and leave them free to follow their self-chosen path.

The great artefacts you see still strewn about your world are the works of these fallen ones. They are evidence of the degree of self-absorption which was overtaking them and diminishing their still mighty powers. The faces on your Easter Island, the huge monuments, the great flight paths built in the hope of drawing us back - these are all theirs and are the means by which they attempted to convince themselves of their glory and the rightness of their cause.

Yet such artefacts are puny compared with what these souls had achieved before. For all their apparent vastness and skill, such monuments are merely the material expression of powers and knowledge which were so much greater in the days of the real glory of the souls involved - before their fall - and it showed how far they had fallen by this time that they took pride in such baubles.

It is equally a measure of how far earth humanity has sunk since then that it marvels at these creations and puzzles over how they were made. Although the fallen ones had descended far into the material by this point, how much further have you fallen into the same pit that so many of you are ignorant of the real means by which these artefacts were produced, and yet pride yourselves on your own childish achievements.

For at that time the fallen ones still had, and still made use of, the power of thought. This is so far from the experience of earth humans today that it is regarded as an impossibility. Fallen people, indeed, who cannot see that thought shapes all, that all is thought! Your thought is made visible all around you in the fatal consequences of your materialism on your world, and in the immense deficit of joy and peace and harmony between you. And still you deny thought's all-embracing creative power.

The fall has been long and hard and very great. We had hoped in the case of a number of our charges that the idyllic surroundings of Earth together with the fact of exile might have the effect of both enticing and shocking them back onto higher paths. We could not force a real reappraisal for that is not the way. But we made the conditions such that reappraisal could be contemplated and embraced. And indeed we had some successes which we welcomed with joy. Those souls were able finally to return to their own people having proved themselves to themselves.

But the rest were so far immersed in their fascination with themselves that this approach could not reach them. Their obsession took them beyond any thoughts of ours. It was through their increasing attempts to play God according to their own debased sense of the Divine, which was caught up with the ego, that their whole edifice was finally brought down.

You keep these events alive in your minds in your faint memories of one particular instance, that of Atlantis. What happened in this case was typical. As the souls involved, in their hubris, attempted to overstep their capabilities with powers which they no longer had the spiritual stature to control, those powers escaped and wrought a tremendous destruction. Everything that had been built was blown irretrievably apart by a furious release of energies which were no longer theirs to use. A great civilisation, which had attracted the brightest, but also the worst, of the fallen ones, sank into the sea.

Not for the first time. In the history of this planet there have been a number of such incidences, of which Atlantis was only the latest - until the present day when once again, as so often before, Earth humanity is attempting to replace Divine Law with its limited, ersatz science.

Some escaped the destruction of Atlantis. These were souls which had not fallen quite so far, as well as others who had incarnated amongst the fallen ones as part of our continuing attempt to the keep the flame of truth burning in the growing darkness.

These souls made their way to numerous corners of the globe and were welcomed by the indigenous peoples, who saw their wisdom and stature and took them for superior beings, for gods.

In this situation, you have to understand that, having separated themselves from the rest of the Universe, the fallen humanities on Earth had by this time brought separation and apartness into all their dealings on this, their own planet. There was very little communication world-wide. Where once all the world was linked through the power of thought, as this declined so the links became tenuous and ultimately intrusive. This development was hastened by the fact that many of the souls whose mission was the wise and compassionate leadership of lesser souls were abandoning their responsibilities in the vain search for greater glory. Thus the lesser peoples were left without the leadership they needed, especially as Atlantis had drawn so many more developed souls like moths to a flame.

When the survivors of Atlantis reached other shores, therefore, their welcome was great. The peoples of these regions learned much from them. They still had great knowledge and they still remembered their origins on other worlds. They built monuments that they might not forget what they had once been and from whence they had come. But the disease of the soul on the planet was so advanced that even the wisest souls could make only partial inroads into its devastation. Indeed, given the nature of the Earth experiment, the devastation could not ultimately be halted, and had to run its course.

Thus great knowledge could not be completely taken in and applied, except in practical matters and some limited spiritual areas. Even where a true outlook was to some extent preserved, as among the North American Indians, the disease was working away in the peoples, and they inevitably declined and fell away from even that wisdom which they still had.

And as they declined, other peoples whose knowledge was less and who had given themselves over to the material to a far greater extent, were able to move in and conquer them and steal their goods and their lands, and their lives.

This was the only possible outcome of the deterioration in the state of being even in the wiser populations. It was already visible, for some time before the Europeans came, in the conflicts between the different tribes in North America; it was solidly entrenched in the peoples of South America, as could be seen in their gruesome rituals; it was evidenced in the peoples in the

Australias as they abandoned their duty of care over their lands and food supplies, and thus their own well-being.

But the decline demonstrated itself most graphically as untruth distorted and twisted the truths by which all lived. Human sacrifice to the gods was a bitter consequence of the lowering of truth to the material from its lofty seat in the spiritual, and was inspired by the fear and the ignorance which comes about when a soul separates itself from its Source. The concentration on the "after-life" among various peoples, most notably the formerly wise Egyptians, was a much diminished understanding of the eternal nature of the human spirit, onto an almost entirely materialistic level. All that was spiritual was gradually reinvented on the material level, and the material reinvention replaced the great truth of which it was only a ghost-like shadow.

For in viewing the eternal, as these souls were still capable of doing until fairly recently despite their growing identification with the material, the fallen ones were looking through a distorting glass, as it might be, and what they saw was no longer an accurate representation of what was there. It was itself a distortion, and these distortions then became the philosophy or understanding of life by which they attempted to live.

They were attempts doomed to failure. As the original impetus of the half-truths faded over time, the distortions themselves were either discarded or the "civilisation" failed through the consequences of its increasing distance from truth, and other "civilisations" then took its place.

This is why so many of the surviving remnants of old knowledge and history are discounted today as myth or legend, or as quaint and primitive customs and ideas. Not only are they of such a different order from the various distortions which took their place, but today's humanity is even less capable of recognising truth, even when it looks them in the eye. In fact, since the last few hundred years of human history on Earth, were truth to look the average human in the eye, he would simply pretend he had not seen something which was so clearly outside all his experience; or he would feel so outraged and threatened at this attack on the fantasy he calls reality that he would complain loudly and bitterly and attempt to destroy whatever or whoever was challenging him in this way.

As you are aware this happens throughout your history, littered as it is with destroyed geniuses whose glimpse of truth was too much for their time. But the truth can never be destroyed or eliminated. What you live in today is actually a mixture of truth and untruth. Where truth is to be found it is rendered safe to your allergic humanity by a mixture of long-established defence mechanisms and a good quantity of familiar untruth. People can then feel comfortable for, after all, what else have they known for uncounted millennia?

You today speak much about truth, and you cling to religions which, even though they may have sprung from truth in the first instance, have inevitably become polluted with the negativity of untruth as the original vision has been worked over by lesser souls.

There is not one of your religions which has not been contaminated by souls immersed in the material. "By their fruits shall ye know them" says your Christian Bible. That is utterly true. The evils perpetrated in the name of the Divine, whether it be called God, or Allah, or Yahweh or Krishna or whatever, testify to the fallen state of spiritual understanding more poignantly than all else. Murder, torture, war, persecution, enslavement, repression, division and atrocities too horrible to describe have nothing whatsoever to do with the harmony and love and peace of the Eternal.

Nor has the greatest negativity that can be perpetrated by any humankind. We mean by this the idea of sin. The Divine has no place for such a concept. Universal Love knows it not.

"Sin" is a purely human, purely material concept. It has no meaning outside your planet. Even upon your planet, fallen as it is, it is an abomination. In all human life in incarnation, there is only experience and learning. No matter how far a soul has fallen from its own lofty reality, no matter how shot through and through with negativity, no matter if it is a channel for negativity as was your Hitler or Stalin, that soul, like every other soul, will eventually find its way back to its Source, its truth, which is that it is a spark of divine fire. It may take some time and much harrowing experience, but nothing can alter that fact. The idea of Hell is an abomination spawned of an abomination.

And indeed, even a Hitler did not enslave a people and deny them the freedom to pursue their own development and truth to the extent of, for example, the highly moral and religious slavers of the American South. Only a materialistic people regards death with the degree of horror it arouses in you. Other humanities feel greater horror at the curtailment of the liberty which is the right of every soul in incarnation. Their emphasis is on the soul where yours is on the body. But it has to be remembered also that in other humanities death is not the often violent and painful procedure it is on Earth, but rather a natural and welcome coming home to the joy of Reality. This also is to be found where the emphasis is on the soul rather than on the soul's temporary vehicle which is all the body really is.

Consider this too: in the palls of blackness amassing on the inner levels on Earth, the negative pressure continually builds and to such a point that, like the volcano which is its outward counterpart, every now and then it has to blow. For this, some kind of conductor is necessary. Hitler and his like were simply conductors for the huge negativity requiring release at the time.

The Second World War appalled many, both then and still today, as the fall-out worked and still works its way through both the unconscious and the conscious awareness of all those involved. Much learning has been facilitated by this single but overwhelming event. Many of those alive today died in that conflict, and many yet need to come to terms with what they experienced then. The shock waves of such an event through time are very great and can dislodge much negative material.

This is to you probably a strange way of understanding things. Were you still identified with eternity and your true eternal being as we are, you would have no difficulty with it. You would know the Spirit as eternal and real, and you would enjoy the game of incarnation as a temporary but important experience and opportunity. You would see how time and events eddy and repeat and renew, and you would understand the wondrous unfolding of the divine plan from another level of consciousness. You would accept reincarnation as a fact of life, and you would know that there is nothing but thought, that indeed all the Universe is thought. You would see that all that seems so solid to you in your everyday lives is in reality gossamer frail, as your own physics has explained, and you would enjoy the process by which thought shapes the material according to its creative design.

The Christian Bible says: "In the beginning was the Word". No, my friends. You in the English-speaking world have been labouring under a mistranslation of the Greek word "logos", which also means "thought". In the beginning was thought.
This was what the fallen ones forgot as they pursued the lure of the material over the long distance from eternity into the temporary and illusory world of time and space. The fall is remembered in fragments of what you call "myth" and "legend". It is the subject of the first book of the Old Testament which tells of the Garden of Eden. The rendering is flawed but the symbolism is accurate, as is the case also with much of the rest of the work.

"Myth" and "legend" record too a golden time - the golden time - before the Fall. They speak of a golden land or Summer Land, for that is what it was. It still exists and all on Earth will one day return to this heaven on Earth - which is quite normal on other planets - in the new world which is coming about. Not all will return to it at the same time, but there will be as many as necessary to propel the creative energy of Spirit in the new world. It is a world of peace, of harmony, of loving co-operation and of increasing identification with the truth of Spirit, which is the true identity of each one.

Thus after millennia of a great crisis of identity, humanity on Earth will regain its crown and radiate once more the light of the Spirit. It will inhabit a radiant world from which all that is negative and of the processes of diminution and dissolution has been purged. The process of separation of positive and negative currently underway is assisting Paradise to come into its own once more on this lovely planet, and a great healing process is spreading its balm over the hurts and divisions of ages. It will be accelerated as those who accept the new world are able to increase their frequency of being towards that of the indwelling Spirit. The absence of negativity will facilitate the rapidity of this raising of frequencies, which has already begun.

We need you to realise the degree to which this humanity has traumatised itself through the crisis of identity which it has itself brought about. In seeking to go one better than the Divine and in setting up materiality in the place of Spirit, Earth people have been rejecting not just the Divine, not just God but their own true Selves, their Source, the Divine within them which is their one and only identity, through which they are at one with All there is, as is the case with every soul.

The fallen ones rejected truth, love, joy and peace along with the truth of their own identity. Thereafter they could not feel happy or contented or joyful on a continuing basis. They experienced the emotional equivalents. What they called happiness or fun often came on a surge of adrenaline; what they called joy too readily poured out of the gaining of some temporary goal on a material level; what they called contentment became increasingly akin to passivity and stagnation.

In separating themselves from their true Selves and its aims, the fallen ones were also cutting themselves off from their inspiration, their direction, their purpose and their meaning. They convinced themselves that their new toys were more meaningful, more true and more to do with their aims. But as the lie inevitably surfaced over the ages, they reacted by dismissing purpose, meaning and harmony altogether as irrelevant, and basing themselves utterly and completely in the material. This was the beginning of what we call the Age of Alienation, and what you call the Enlightenment or the Age of Reason, in which science threw in its lot with the material by basing itself solely on measurement and verification.

The identification of science with the material gave birth to the modern age, the industrial age, the age of technology, the age of increasing alienation of humanity, both from itself and from the world it had fashioned. This was expressed finally, not far from the lowest point of earth history, in terms of alienation from God. God was declared dead! We who observed and who have always helped and supported the positive in your negative world experienced much amusement at this, as you would experience at the naiveté of the pronouncements of your children.

It was however the logical outcome of the original rejection of their true identity by the fallen ones. With the industrial age came the lowest possible expression of the identification with the material. The process of separation from Self, from nature and from the Universe accelerated rapidly. Where God was not rejected outright, He became more a reflection of the ego concerns of His followers than what He truly is. And this is understandable. God made man in His image. But man on Earth has re-fashioned God in his own debased image as he has fallen from his oneness with the Divine.

What this has led to is the increasing anxiety of humanity and the increasing trivialisation of its aims and efforts. It has written its inherent conflict with itself large upon its world. Where humanity lived once in harmony with nature, for example, in mutual cooperation, nature has become the enemy, something to be attacked and tamed and exploited. The natural world on Earth reflects humanity back to itself in its pollution, its violent attacks on human beings through storm and flood and fire and pestilence, all of which are the consequences of humanity's own actions towards nature.

This situation can be likened to a beautiful flower, whose petals are marvels of colour and texture, each with its place and each contributing to the pleasing design of the whole flower, but where one of the petals attempts to combat its fellows and the flower of which it is part and subdue them to its own idea of how the flower should be. You would think that such a petal is quite mad, and of course in the same way so is a humanity that is sustained by a wonderful, rich and fertile natural world when it attempts to impose its own feeble and mistaken ideas upon its environment and sustenance, rather than working with that environment to achieve its aims.

It is sad to see such a wanton waste of resources and the resulting decimation of the planet's natural riches. It is rather more amusing to see how humanity's conflict with itself is projected in its attitudes to the rest of the Universe and its depiction of "aliens" and invasions and attacks from space. From space, dear ones, comes only love and joy and great peace. But so ruled are you by fear that you cannot see nor feel the truth. You can only see what you fear in everything.

Your inheritance today from the countless ages of negativity is this fear which cuts you off from all that is real and meaningful and joyful. In many cases, whole populations are living only to survive; in others, it is to gain as much as possible on the material level; while in yet others, life is a matter simply of fending off despair and fear by all means possible, including the most superficial of occupations and past-times and thoughts, or the most terrible atrocities against other human beings.

You might think we paint too black a picture. But just think for a moment of what has been perpetrated throughout your history. Think of the wasted creative energies, the missed opportunities to love, to contribute, to enhance life for Self and others; think of what human history could have been - a joyful participation in a golden world in loving friendship and cooperation with other worlds.

For, in cutting himself off from his true Self, Earth man has also closed the door on communication with other humanities and the Oneness of the Universe. Think of your lives as they could be now - creative, relaxed, joyful and full of a sense of belonging to a vast and loving whole, full of wonder and marvels with no wars, no violence, no stress - and of course no aliens! Yet the picture is not completely black. Its gloom is shot through with gleams of purest light wherever great souls have blazed a trail for liberty and inspiration through their unshakeable commitment to the truth within them.

They kept faith despite often severely debilitating emotional traumas and disabilities and in the most adverse of circumstances. They kept alive the flame of truth and, wherever they could, brought light and a way forward through the negativity and stagnation of earth conditions. At times a group would come together in an enterprise of such light that the flame would blaze across the entire history of the globe such as in the founding of the United States of America or the writing of the plays of Shakespeare. At other times, the power of light in one soul could achieve the seemingly impossible as did Churchill in the dark hopelessness of Britain's situation in the Second World War.

Great prophets have brought the light of truth to men; great artists and musicians and poets have touched the light in many hearts through the sheer power of their inspiration. And although the light has been all too often hijacked by darkness for its dismal ends, yet truth survives unscathed like nuggets of gold in dark ore. Throughout the ages it has shown a way to souls who seek, and it has thrown into sharp relief the poverty of the negative so that, like the grit in the oyster, it has irritated the souls of those involved until they turned their energies into more constructive directions.

This is now the time of healing. In these last days before the new world, all of you who have chosen to join it are finding that you are being borne along by a new energy and purpose. There is a need to come to terms with the detritus of the old world which still irritates and impedes the soul's longing to progress.
Anxiety and fear and frustration and disease need to be understood for what they are, so that they may be discarded along with all that is negative in the world that has been - and is now beginning to pass.

We hope that our thoughts in this book will help in this process of transformation and renewal, so that you may come closer to us and our love and peace and joy, and thus to the love and peace and joy within yourselves.

Out of this the new world, the golden age, will arise once more on your lovely planet, and the Universe entire will be at peace.

Extra Terrestrial

7/10/98

FREE DETAILED CATALOGUE

Everything You Always Wanted To Know About Your Body, But So Far Nobody's Been Able To Tell You, Chris Thomas & D Baker
Face of the Deep - Healing Body & Soul, Penny Allen
Fairies in the Irish Tradition, Molly Gowen
Fool's First Steps, (The) Chris Thomas
From Past to Future Life, Dr Roger Webber
Gardening For Wildlife Ron Wilson
Goddess on the Cross, Dr George Young
Handbook For Pagan Healers, Liz Joan
Handbook of Fairies, Ronan Coghlan
Healing Book, The, Chris Thomas and Diane Baker
Healing Homes, Jennifer Dent
Healing Journeys, Paul Williamson
Healing Stones, Sue Philips
Herb Craft - Shamanic & Ritual Use of Herbs, Lavender & Franklin
In Search of Herne the Hunter, Eric Fitch
Inner Space Workbook - Develop Thru Tarot, C Summers & J Vayne
Intuitive Journey, Ann Walker Isis - African Queen, Akkadia Ford
Journey Home, The, Chris Thomas
Language of the Psycards, Berenice
Legend of Robin Hood, The, Richard Rutherford-Moore
Living Tarot, Ann Walker
Lore of the Sacred Horse, Marion Davies
Lost Lands & Sunken Cities (2nd ed.), Nigel Pennick
Magic of Herbs - A Complete Home Herbal, Rhiannon Ryall
Magical Guardians - Exploring the Spirit and Nature of Trees, Philip Heselton
Magical History of the Horse, Janet Farrar & Virginia Russell
Magical Lore of Animals, Yvonne Aburrow
Magical Lore of Cats, Marion Davies
Magical Lore of Herbs, Marion Davies
Masks of Misrule - Horned God & His Cult in Europe, Nigel Jackson
Medicine For The Coming Age, Lisa Sand MD
Medium Rare - Reminiscences of a Clairvoyant, Muriel Renard
Mind Massage - 60 Creative Visualisations, Marlene Maundrill
Mystic Life of Animals, Ann Walker
Patchwork of Magic - Living in a Pagan World, Julia Day
Pathworking - A Practical Book of Guided Meditations, Pete Jennings
Personal Power, Anna Franklin
Places of Pilgrimage and Healing, Adrian Cooper
Practical Divining, Richard Foord
Practical Meditation, Steve Hounsome
Practical Spirituality, Steve Hounsome
Psychic Self Defence - Real Solutions, Jan Brodie
Real Fairies, David Tame
Reality - How It Works & Why It Mostly Doesn't, Rik Dent
Romany Tapestry, Michael Houghton
Runic Astrology, Nigel Pennick

Sacred Animals, Gordon MacLellan
Sacred Celtic Animals, Marion Davies, Ill. Simon Rouse
Sacred Dorset - On the Path of the Dragon, Peter Knight
Sacred Grove - The Mysteries of the Forest, Yvonne Aburrow
Sacred Geometry, Nigel Pennick
Sacred Nature, Ancient Wisdom & Modern Meanings, A Cooper
Season of Sorcery - On Becoming a Wisewoman, Poppy Palin
Secret Signs & Sigils, Nigel Pennick
Self Enlightenment, Mayan O'Brien
Spirits of the Air, Jaq D Hawkins
Spirits of the Earth, Jaq D Hawkins
Spirits of the Earth, Jaq D Hawkins
Stony Gaze, Investigating Celtic Heads John Billingsley
Stumbling Through the Undergrowth , Mark Kirwan-Heyhoe
Subterranean Kingdom, The, revised 2nd ed, Nigel Pennick
Symbols of Ancient Gods, Rhiannon Ryall
Talking to the Earth, Gordon MacLellan
Taming the Wolf - Full Moon Meditations, Steve Hounsome
Teachings of the Wisewomen, Rhiannon Ryall
The Other Kingdoms Speak, Helena Hawley
Tree: Essence of Healing, Simon & Sue Lilly
Tree: Essence, Spirit & Teacher, Simon & Sue Lilly
Through the Veil, Peter Paddon
Understanding Chaos Magic, Jaq D Hawkins
Vortex - The End of History, Mary Russell
Warp and Weft - In Search of the I-Ching, William de Fancourt
Warriors at the Edge of Time, Jan Fry
Water Witches, Tony Steele
Way of the Magus, Michael Howard
Weaving a Web of Magic, Rhiannon Ryall
West Country Wicca, Rhiannon Ryall
Wildwitch - The Craft of the Natural Psychic, Poppy Palin
Wildwood King , Philip Kane
Witches of Oz, Matthew & Julia Philips
Wondrous Land - The Faery Faith of Ireland by Dr Kay Mullin
Working With the Merlin, Geoff Hughes
Your Talking Pet, Ann Walker